SUFFOLK HOURS

BY THE SAME AUTHOR

Via Ypres (*A Record of the Field Ambulances 39 Div. B. E. F.*)
Suffolk Yesterdays
This Suffolk
North-east Suffolk
Household and Country Crafts
An Hour-glass on the Run
A Window in Suffolk
Under a Suffolk Sky
A Suffolk Calendar
In Suffolk Borders
The Felixstowe Story
Suffolk Remembered
Suffolk Villages
Victorian Suffolk
Portrait of Suffolk
Suffolk Miscellany
The Creeping Hours of Time
Something of Old Suffolk

SUFFOLK HOURS

Allan Jobson

ROBERT HALE · LONDON

First published in Great Britain 1979

ISBN 0 7091 7621 X

Robert Hale Limited
Clerkenwell House
Clerkenwell Green
London, EC1R 0HT

Photoset, printed and bound
in Great Britain by
REDWOOD BURN LIMITED
Trowbridge & Esher

Contents

Illustrations

For
my youngest
Grandchild
Benjamin Allan Jobson

To Suffolk

When robins fed their spotted young,
And catkins from the hazels hung;
When warbler flaunting warbler sung,
And squirrels on the pine-trees hung;
When days were bright, and skies were blue,
And yokels 'gan again to woo;
When thrush and blackbird early woke,
And leaves had bronzed upon the oak;
Said I, now cheerless days are done,
My pilgrimage shall be begun.
Yet here I stay and years go by,
And Suffolk knows the reason why.

Cecil H. Lay (1885–1956)
Suffolk Countryman, Painter, Poet and Architect

Foreword

There is a continuing satisfaction in reading about old country life; yesterday has a charm about it, particularly the landscape–"Where trees half check the light with trembling shades". There was certainly a fragrance about the countryside when I was a boy that we have lost today. Although I sometimes catch it when I go for my post-prandial walk and pass a sweet-briar hedge; it greets me yards away with its evocation of memories. In Suffolk the poppies predominated everywhere and were such a glorious sight in the hedgerows and amongst the ripening corn. They also grew in Flanders fields.

Those poor old folk lived a hard life but generally, as far as Suffolk was concerned, a happy and contented one. Perhaps you will say because they knew no other. My grandfather was born in the 'twenties or 'thirties of last century, and must have passed through the varying chances and changes of agricultural fortunes. But I never once heard him complain. I spoke of this to one I knew as a village girl, a year older than myself. Her reply was: "Neither did my father and what was more, we were never allowed to complain about the weather as that was in the hands of God." Whether we like to admit it or not, their religion was the secret of their contentment. It was not an opiate as some would suggest.

My grandparents' old chapel at Middleton, which they loved, has just celebrated its 150th anniversary. In turning out old papers for their little exhibition, I discovered that my mother's people had been there years before it was built. So they must have been amongst those who rejoiced when the doors were first opend for the service of thanksgiving singing those great hymns of the Wesleys.

Lord Home in his *The Way the Wind Blows* declares himself on the side of the angels. He asked Harold Macmillan if he could put his finger on the point of time when the slide in values in Britain began. The answer may seem strange to many but it came without hesitation "The day when people stopped going to Church regularly on a Sunday morning."

I think it is true to say that the spirit of Suffolk is kept alive today by the Aldeburgh Festival, with its annual programme of music and the arts. For long enough the visual arts have flourished in Suffolk, and now music has been added by the late Lord Britten, OM., CH., giving the still unspoilt Victorian Aldeburgh a world-wide fame. Benjamin Britten lies in a simple grave on the north side of Aldeburgh Church.

1

Our Village

Now sign your names, which shall be read,
Mute symbols of a joyful morn,
By village eyes as yet unborn.
The names are signed and overhead.

Dear Christine,

We have found the most lovely place in which to live and die. Curiously enough it is between the sea and the churchyard. The town itself, but for the distinction of a post office, bus station, telephone exchange and an ancient fire station, might be mistaken for a village. In fact it is very much in the nature of a village, because it is full of characters, and there is always a bit of scandal floating about. After all, what is life without something to whisper about and enjoy. As someone has said, "Every man is as God hath made him, and sometimes a great deal worse".

I think we are very fortunate in our timing, I mean before all these individuals are blown away and robots take their place. As it is, a super-market has made its appearance and all the little shops are going self-service. Some are hoping the chemists will go that way too, so that one can buy (or purloin) pep pills without so much fuss being made about them. And, of course, bearded weirdies are making their appearance, in spite of such an advance in our plumbing systems, and the low price of soap.

We have one or two main roads: one goes right through what is euphemistically called the town centre; another goes to the grim outskirts that end in the sea and our docks, where are our gold and opal mines. Another goes to a very ancient place, known as the ferry. This latter is the home of the aborigines. Bitter about the loss of their rights, stolen they say by the local authorities, these people live alone, always looking out to sea and complaining about the state of their sea wall and wondering if they will get swamped.

However, two, three or four times a day, a delightful person takes his life in his hand, starts up his engine and sets off for the hazards of our civilized parts. He and his period bus are so well known that grandchildren hail him as he passes by, "There goes Uncle's bus!" There are certain persons that seem as though they could go on for ever, and he is one. You pay your fourpence as you go in, help yourself to any change, and settle down to listen to the conversation, because everyone knows about everyone else. It is a sort of Mrs Wilson's Diary.

There has been a movement to bring back the village school. It has even grown into a National Association for the Support of Small Schools, an organization campaigning against the wholesale closure by the Government of village schools. One spokesman, Dr Rhodes Boyson, said that village, and other small schools had generally high standards. "I went to a village school from five to nine and look back with pleasure at the sound education and security I obtained."

Is it too late to bring back this village background to a life, giving a locality and a home to look back upon? Too many of these once centres of life have been closed in Suffolk, and children taken miles away for their upbringing, to their great loss of individuality.

True, we cannot go back on the tracks of time, but we need not all be cast in one mould like coins of the realm. The old days were full of individuals and their faces live to cheer our memory. The 'penny plain' are forgotten and it is the 'tuppence coloured' that stand out. Such as great-grandmother, who wore a large black poke bonnet, a blue cloak and carried a huge gig umbrella for safety's sake, not only for the rain but for use against anything that might attack her. It must have been a relation of hers, as told by an old Suffolk parson, who declared: "No he don't, he shan't hev no more bacca in this world! He led me a dance last night, he wouldn't lie down till I made him; an' all through that bacca. So there's an end on't!" And yet another relation who was quick to reply when her husband struck out, "Where are ye? I'm a dyin!", "Whoi, ye auld fule, didn't yer tell me afore I got me things off."

The old gardener comes to kindly remembrance who was great on the cultivation of potatoes; but his maxim on the subject of flowers was "Weed 'em well, an' let 'em bide." And of a good harvest, "Ah, bor, there'll be plenty o' baulk t' year."

This leads me to the local garage proprietor. (Of course, there are more than one.) He is really wonderful. He is an old bird, but you wouldn't think it, and delights in a winter and summer plumage. We haven't been here long, but we have seen both. I like his summer dress best. It consists of shorts that come down to just above his knees, so that one gets a full view of a pair of legs that appear as though they had just been plucked. His hat is of the pork-pie variety, caked so thick with oil and grease as though overdone in a hot kiln. He laughs and sings, is always running to his till, knows everyone for miles around, can tell you who was and who wasn't, but finds it difficult to assess who is and who isn't. As he would remark if he knew the lines,

> All are scattered now and fled,
> Some are married, some are dead.

Then we have a public figure who has presided over our poor destinies more than once, so I am told. When his car is out of action, he progresses along our main thoroughfare. Progress is the right word, for a more upright, stately figure and march could only be equalled by a Guards officer. He dresses according to inclination and will. I met him once in our train, wearing a bowler hat that looked the oddest thing in men's wear, just sitting on his head. Sometimes it is a wide-awake, like Uncle Sam's, or a type that was worn in the Crimea. He is a big man, moves in a big way, has a genial, boyish face, and might be heard to say,

> I cannot draw a cart, nor eat dried oats:
> If it be man's work, I'll do it.

Of doctors we have a score. There may be a dearth of these men elsewhere, but we have plenty here. In fact, we are aiming at one for every street. They are really all hand-picked, of whom it might be said,

> Knowledge is proud that he has learned so much;
> Wisdom is humble that he knows no more.

But it's the very devil if you're taken ill at night. Indeed, " 'Tis a naughty night to swim in." For gone are the days when he leaps from his bed into an icy bedroom, opens the window, and is scarcely awake 'ere he find himself lacing his boots, and preparing to saddle his horse, or draw out his motor, and hurry off to his afflicted patient. Needless to say, they all go in cars, and it is said they can be distinguished one from another by their driving. One goes round corners on two wheels, but nearly all stop at the traffic lights.

There is one in particular, soft of speech, roomy of girth, who seems to hold fate and physic in his hands. You pour out your troubles like a creaking door, thinking it is a tale you only can tell, although in reality he has heard it all before. Yet his cheery manner, bright looks and encouraging words have coaxed many back to life and health again.

> But to each one he said,
> You will quickly be dead,
> If you don't take these pills fifty times a day.

He is by way of being what is known in Suffolk as a 'crowner'; although in all fairness, he was not the gentleman at a Suffolk inquest who asked questions by the book. There had been a railway accident, and a woman killed at a railway crossing. The driver of the train explained that on examining the line he discovered the trunk of the poor victim on one side of the line and the lower part of the body on the other. "And was the deceased dead when you found her?" asked the coroner.

Do you remember what Cotgrave says of one of these gentlemen in his *Treasury of Wit and Language*? He writes of a certain Dr Pulsefeel, who claimed that he could make all the women beautiful, rectify the body, clarify the blood, perfume your skin, tinct your hair, enliven your eye, heighten your appetite without detriment to your waist line, and supply wondrous things in the way of jellies, dentifrices, pomatums etc.

Remember too, it was a Dr Bullayn, who lived at Blaxhall nearby, who in his *Book of Simples*, recommends the use of sage and daisy tea for gout and rheumatism. And pearl mixture – which contained white pearls, sapphire, jacinth, cornelian, emeralds, basil, mace, coral, amber, shavings of ivory, ginger, pepper, spikenard, thin pieces of gold and silver, musk and honey. These were good things for diseases of the brain, heart and stomach. "King and nobles have used this for their comfort. It causeth them to be bold-spirited, the body to smell well, and engendereth to the face a good colour." But I can assure you he was not the first quack.

> Canst thou not minister to a mind diseased,
> Pluck from the memory a rooted sorrow,
> Raze out the written troubles of the brain,
> And with some sweet oblivious antidote
> Cleanse the stuffed bosoms of that perilous stuff
> Which weighs upon the heart.

However, I am given to understand on good authority that

one of the most important divisions of mankind is between the eupeptic and the dyspeptic. We have both here.

Of parsons also we have great store because, I understand, there is something in seaside air which attracts the race. Some come here on the last lap to heaven, others for the purpose of keeping out of the same as long as possible. But all have their definite routes mapped out, determined by the colleges of their training. I think I might quote you the famous lines on this,

And not by eastern windows only
When daylight comes, comes in the light.

Have you ever thought that most people's ideas of heaven, don't go much farther back than their grandparents? Gone are the days of sermon tasting, but it is only discovered what miracles of oratory their sermons were, when the preacher dies or moves to another parish. Hindsight is a tremendous advantage where the pulpit is concerned.

In arguing, too, the parson owned his skill,
For e'en though vanquished, he could argue still.

Yet we have to admit in some few instances,

He's a rare man,
Our parson; half a head above us all.

As for me,

I neither know nor care
Whether a parson ought to wear
A black dress or a white dress
Filled with troubles of my own,
A wife who preaches in her gown,
And lectures in her night-dress.

And do you know, Christine, we have a couple of carriers

who ply between here and our county town. This is a survival from the distant past if you like, when the old hooded carts lumbered along the rutty roads carrying goods and persons. Considering the state of our roads, it was a perilous undertaking; but they survived, and folks enjoyed it. The big wagons would have as many as four horses, while the one-horsed affairs were drawn by poor old things that had usually gone over at the knees. When it was a case of going up hill, passengers had to get out and walk.

To climb steep hills
Requires slow pace at first.

The older carrier of our two started when Queen Victoria was celebrating her jubilee. He and his hoss would jog along those awful roads, come wind, come weather, always with his eye cocked to see if anyone wanted him to call for a parcel, or to bring back a package. He might be greeted thus: "Are yew a-goin' to Edwardse's or Footman's? If so be would yew bring me back a pair o' butes? Don't forgit I've got a bunion on me left foot, and me big toe on me right foot fare tew be out o' the true. Bring back a nice roomy pair, if yew plaise."

"Oh, and by the way, I could dew with tew yards o' tape, an' a new hat. I've only got a small hid, if me feet are large. But I 'ont trouble you about a pair o' stockings. I'll git them meself when I hap to gew there."

Of course the journey took all day, a long day at that. It started early and finished late. Sometimes Thomas had a few unpaid passengers. Boys, even old boys, would wait in the hedges for the familiar old cart, let it get on a bit, and then run out and sit on the axle, to help them on the road home. Tom would appear not to notice, and then in his Suffolk high-pitched voice, exclaim, "I know yew're there, together."

Occasionally, he would bring home a real live passenger, a little owd mawther, to spend a holiday with her grandmother. On arrival he would tie up his mare, take the child by the hand

and deliver her safe and sound to Mrs Keeble, or old Mrs Catchpole. And on being asked, how much that was? reply, "That'll be thrippence, ma'am, if yew plaize."

But he must have had wagons as well, because in the summer, when he was not so busy, he used to cater for Sunday School treats. As everyone went to Sunday School in those days, and if they played truant at other times of the year, they didn't round about treat times or Christmas, so there must have been a whole jorum of them. The wagons would be all dressed up, the horses likewise, and they would jog off, as far as Waldringfield or Levington or even Nacton. What with a ride in the wagon, a thumping good tea, butter put on the bread so that you could see it, cakes, buns, rusks, apples and what not, it must have been something to remember and talk about.

Time moves on, whether we will or no, and just before the Great War, Thomas bought himself one of the very first motor vehicles to be seen in our streets. That was enterprise for you if you like. Who would have thought of a country carrier driving one of those old things. It whooly spluttered and hissed along, frightening the horses, scaring the women in their gossips and scattering the old hens. It was a two-cylinder, chain-driven Wolseley, and rocked from side to side as it galloped along at five miles an hour, without stopping for bait at the Hand in Hand.

Come five years later he had two boys in the business. The war was over, and they managed to get some solid-tyred lorries and ran a regular haulage business. Meanwhile, the speed limit had grown to twenty miles an hour, but they couldn't make it. They would have rattled themselves to pieces if they had.

That old carrier's business still runs on, a daily reminder of long ago. It is run by his grandson, but he doesn't do the running himself.

The one carrier's initial is 'N.' and the other 'B' so between them they make up a 'mark well, take notice'. And whereas one stays at home, the other, with his son, sallies forth every morning, a genteel, kindly pair, of whose like it would be difficult to find. Courtesy is a gentle flavour, not always to be found in the 11-plus syllabus, but we have it here. The son is in our choir, so I know.

I could tell you of others – of a retired Police Inspector, into whose arms it must have been a privilege to fall. I feel sure he must have made his arrests with an apology for interfering with one's freedom, especially if it was a drunken woman. And there is a gentleman, I use the word advisedly, who deals with rats, wasps' nests and vermin in general. He too is of the guinea stamp.

Then we have a removal contractor, whom I will call Charlie. He is a character if ever there was one. His roots go back a long way in this village, to when you had to live and die here, doff your cap to the squire and his relations, and mind you didn't get in the way of the curate. Charlie worked for his father who, like a lot more, kept horses. A rare lot of people here started that way, going about four miles an hour and being contented, even if they have risen to fifty and sixty miles an hour in their old age, birking at thirty through the built-up areas. He says he was paid three pence a week and a kick up the behind, although he used a different word, that was often on Chaucer's lips. As you are hoping to take English at A level, you would know the term.

This didn't suit him at all, and he told his mother so: "I've had enough o' that!" So he announced his intention of hiking off to Australia. But if his father was a tough lot his mother had a soft spot for her boy. She offered to buy him a carriage and pair if he would stay at home. And like a wise lad he did.

A carriage and pair all his own. What more could an enterprising lad want? True the old carriage had iron tyres to its wheels, real leather for the upholstery, a couple of lamps that burnt candles and went out in windy weather, together with a whip that stood up in a holder. And a pair of the thinnest horses to be seen for miles around. You will understand that he used this contrivance in the same way as we use a taxi to-day. He would run people about in all directions, clip-clop, and did a roaring trade with visitors.

Wonderful old things those affairs were, smelling of grease, dust, leather and stockholm tar. And, complying with the laws of the land, he wore an enamel tag with a number on it near his watch-chain, while another was fixed to the back of the carriage. So far so good, but father living up to his reputation wouldn't allow Charles to stable the horses at home, so he had to use one of our famous inns, that stood on our sea front, and was made of wood. The son was equal to the mother's trust.

And so Charles grew up, bought a pony and van, and began to do cartage jobs. It was the first step to household removals, a fleet of vans that look like morgues on wheels, and distance no object. Unlike his long dead parent, Charles can say with Shakespeare,

> Therefore my age is as a lusty winter
> Frosty but kindly.

Of grocers we have one or more, some began small and grew big; others small have grown smaller. One of the latter asked me if I had an old pair of trousers I could give him, which fortunately I had. May I quote you the immortal lines, and leave it at that,

> When the grocer's made his pile,
> Does he grow nicer?
> No sir, he does not change his heart and style
> But grows a grosser grocer.

Just one thing more, did you see that little bit in the *Telegraph* recently? "At table, Victoria, aged nine, to Adelaide, six, who was briskly shaking nutmeg on her tapioca pudding: 'You know you can get fixed on nutmeg, Adelaide.'"

So goodbye for now, Christine.

From your aged and senile Parent.

2

A Last Look

Who may regret what was, since it has made
Himself, himself?

John Freeman

I said at first I would never go back, it should remain a pious memory. I was too old. Then one evening I announced to my wife: "We will go back. Let it be tomorrow." And tomorrow it was.

We were soon on the old familiar train to Liverpool Street Station, then by bus over the new London Bridge to that station. But it was not the station we had always known, although we found the old familiar platform and a train waiting beside that rather grim dividing wall. And then came dear old Anerley Station. It might have been a ghost train, not a soul to be seen and the only way out by the little tunnel that led to the up-side. I thought, as we descended, of the bad old days on our way to school when it became a byword for grime and dirt. Then we lost the short cut and had to go over the bridge.

Our feet naturally found old St Hugh's Road. What a transformation! The last time I had seen it, the bulldozer was at work. Now all was new, wonderfully new, in a complex that allowed pedestrians only, little bridges leading from one block of flats to another, and sundry little grass plots, even parking places for cars. Yet there was something missing; the silence of respectability had given place to the pulsating life of the old days.

Indeed, there was not a sign of life, not even a baby carriage to suggest a rising generation. I could not but think of the old order, when folks gathered on their doorsteps to watch the fun. The little woman with her white apron who had a voice that would penetrate to the remote distances as she shouted after her one and only, "Frankie! Frankie!" Frankie would hear if he couldn't be seen and would respond; woe betide him if he didn't. And there were no boys on perambulator wheels, steering their box into the girls skipping, with a "sling yer hook!" as they sped on.

In those old grubby days it was wonderful how boys would try to find some bit of locomotion, perchance a worn out bicycle, as they took advantage of the slope of the road: Which set me wondering what happened to the boy opposite, son of a very disreputable family. He fell off his rickety machine and received a terrible gash on his cheek. But my mother came to the rescue, called him in and bathed the wound at our sink. Which was the sort of thing she would do.

Now everything was so respectable. So we made our way amongst the little terraces nearby, that had been there all the time, noting that the mission room had gone. We turned our backs on the unsaintly St Hugh's Road that had become so respectable and in so doing a bit characterless. Yet the building of the old street was of no great antiquity, since mother took her first baby there, born in Middleton, her Suffolk home, to a new little home in 1878. Come to think of it, just a century ago.

As the station was in the charge of the lowest possible denominator – one – we decided to eat our sandwiches on the platform. We sat in full view of the pub that stood at the end of the cab rank on the opposite side of the station. But how those trains thundered through! No plumes of smoke or shrill whistles. The little pseudo-Elizabethan house beside the entrance to the station was still there, but no station master with gold braid to supervise, with a certain amount of pride, his spotless charge. And wild growth had overrun that little bank where the wild flowers and the grasses grew.

Then came the reflection, "Wouldn't it be nice if we could go and see the house where we started married life?" Of course it would, but that meant climbing the little hill past the small shops that were, alas, in a bad way. It might have been said also about that other parade, where the chemist had his proprietary lamp-post; the dairy where you could get a glass of milk for a penny; and another where the smell of roasting coffee-beans suggested a morning's gossip. However, a bus took us up that little climb for about 1s. 6d old money, instead of the nimble penny.

Yes it was still there, that tall house of such happy memories, where we sojourned on the top floor; just ourselves. Then came the remark, "Just look at those steps that Mildred kept so white!" Was Mildred still alive we wondered? And as we were so near I suggested we should go and see if the house was still there, where my mother, in her teens, came as a maid from her village home in Suffolk.

Here again came a great surprise, not of newness of desolation, but of old world beauty. The little wooden cottage tucked away in the corner had gone, but there seemed little of change. And over there was the old house! Most beautifully kept, it seemed hardly real, so we sat on the trunk of a tree opposite to enjoy it. I almost wondered if I should see my mother come tripping out from that sideway on her way to climb that so steep hill to meet her young man who was to be my father. He would be waiting by the chapel on the top of another steep hill, of course. This all provided a reward for that last look.

I was to find out later, that all that area had formed part of Hayes Farm, cultivated by a man named Ruskin, who could claim relationship with the famous John; and the little wooden house that had disappeared was where he lived.

Neither did we overlook that lovely little oasis in the stream of life, labelled Palace Gardens. So reminiscent of that great monster of glass removed from Hyde Park, and a memorial to the ever planning and progressive brain of the Prince Consort. Not forgetting Handel Festivals, and a sight of Clara Butt standing on a red carpet wearing an orange costume!

But we had to leave this bosky dell and pass on, remembering it was indeed a half-pay neighbourhood, with houses given reflective names such as Azim Ghur, Dapoonie Villa, Malabar Lodge, Coogee House, Nassau Villa; and where one short, select little road held at one and the same time a major-general, admiral, captain and a colonel. They had been members of the old army with memories of Waterloo, the Crimea and the Mutiny. I am afraid they were a hard lot, their exploits accomplished on the old black powder.

So we made our way down that Hamlet Road to find our parish church of St Paul's (whose vicar at one time had enough sons and nephews at Dulwich College to form a cricket team) had been pulled down, but a note stated that a new one was to be erected on the site.

So we continued down Anerley Road, past all kinds of memories and those once very high-class shops, over Anerley Bridge, down Station Road to Oakfield Road which was as like a battlefield as was possible in peace time. Gone were the little shops, even pubs and a board school, with one of the groves blocked up. So to Beckenham Road, not so greatly altered, to the famous Crooked Billet, of which you can read in Hone's *Table Book*, to the old police station still functioning with its blue lamp, recalling memories of drunks and others, being wheeled in on a full length hand ambulance. True they had the decency to provide a hood that could be pulled over the head, so that the person's identity was hidden, and only feet left dangling to show the sex.

Here we crossed over to pass where the old school stood, that had lived a good and wholesome life of some eighty-seven years, to catch a bus that took us direct to that Elmers End cemetery of morbid memory. Fortified by a cup of tea we entered. When near the grave what a sight there was of the most vicious overgrowth, like something out of the tropics. I found the grave at last, falling over in the process amid the spiked growth.

One thing achieved, but it set me philosophizing on the folly of those elaborate memorials that serve but a turn. For as I walked those grass-grown paths I noticed that the grave of our old vicar, although of marble, was fast developing into the same condition. So we turned our backs on old obsequies and came home from that Norwood Junction, once the scene of so many signal lights that we could watch flashing from our Anerley Bridge.

I mentioned in my *Autobiography* that a neighbouring parish housed Dr Conan Doyle the famous creator of Sherlock Holmes. It was with something of surprise that I read that his father Charles Altmond Doyle was the son of an artist, one of four brothers who had artistic talents. The best known was Richard Doyle, particularly celebrated for his drawings in *Punch* in the mid-Victorian period. Charles was a civil servant in the Scottish Office of Works. Later in life he was kept in the Montrose Royal Lunatic Asylum, not because he was insane, but rather as an alcoholic and subject to epileptic fits. His drinking drove him into fits of madness, and in one of these, together with an epileptic fit, he died. Conan Doyle was supposed to have made contact with his father after death through spiritualism.

In the old days they said our street in south-east London, indeed the whole neighbourhood with the exception of a few sequestered roads, was noisy. But what about our Suffolk home on a sunlit morning when the American jets fly over? True we are out of the pathway of Concorde, yet our skies are streaked with sound. No longer does the woodpecker use our lawn, or the wandering voice of the cuckoo harbinger the spring. As for the lark, it has become extinct as far as we are concerned. However, we must be thankful that the robin has not deserted us, or the blackbirds, or the timid thrush. They are still our friends if they do rob us of any soft fruit we might have. And sometimes we can stand and wonder at that marvel of creation, a thing of ineffable beauty, a dragon fly, pendant in the air. What a lovely sight which vanishes as suddenly as it appears. Progress and expansion has but little thought of these things.

3

Lament for Gaslight

For this and that way swings
The flux of mortal things,
Though moving inly to one far-set goal.
After light's term, a term of cecity.
Matthew Arnold

On looking back through the vista of the years it is difficult to decide whether sunshine or shadow dominates the scene. It has been said that the summers of childhood were always fine, but I am not sure about that. One's circumstance of birth might affect it.

Our street was lit by gaslight, but also by sunlight, and I can see the picture now which each in turn gave to the slope of the pavements and the little houses that lined the way. Indeed, our whole lives were lit by gaslight, and in comparison with modern lighting were that much the softer. Sunlight on the other hand was apt to accentuate the drabness and make the cracks in the stucco more apparent, besides bringing out the smells and giving wing to the flies. There were not many of these little iron standards, with bulging bases, in the street, but they were fitting heirs to the village pump and were all true vintage models, giving what we then thought a sufficiency of light from the top end to the dim recess at the bottom.

The lamp-lighter, of happy memory, came down our street with his magic stick, but he is long since dead. Did they bury his fire-laden stick, as we buried father's crutch, when they took him to Elmers End? Fitting emblems of the end of an era.

There were of course other uses for our lamp-standards. Apart from being community centres, the bases were used for a number of pastimes belonging to youth, including acting as a home for tig. Some enterprising young rascal might climb up that gentle stem and dowse the gleam, when it would be very dark, then swing on the cross bar before dropping to earth and scampering off into the encircling gloom.

On looking back, I suppose that dim lighting made the fireworks at the Palace the more splendid. I think it was the 'spider' that gave me a certain vertiginous feeling as its legs spread across the darkness, searching perhaps for me. But the rockets were just splendid, filling the sky with bouquets of colour, like burning hundreds-and-thousands. It is a funny thing how grown-ups adore fireworks, especially Old Etonians.

And then I think of my old bedroom that was at the top of the house, facing the station platform and a fine rowan tree, with a view of chimney pots across the railway lines. I became possessed of an old deal table with a drawer, covered it with green baize and used it to improve my mind. How often did I sit there and dream dreams of becoming this or that in spite of drawbacks.

In a recess by the fireplace a row of open shelves (they cost me a shilling) held the books I had acquired. These included Forster's *Life of Charles Dickens* in two volumes, Livingstone's *Last Journals,* and a book entitled *Mr Livingstone, I Presume?* and an American edition of Milton's *Works,* illustrated. I also had *Lloyd's Encyclopaedic Dictionary* which I had bought in unbound numbers at a penny each and bound up myself. If I remember aright, the old bookseller noticed I was collecting these up by degrees, so he put up the price. I had to work by candlelight, after I had left work at 8 p.m.

It is a curious fact that mother's East Anglia seemed to dominate our part of South East London, certainly from a religious point of view, in the name of Spurgeon. He must have been an extraordinary young man whose stewards could not find a place large enough to hold his congregations. So in the end they built the Metropolitan Tabernacle, Newington Butts, which he used to fill. And this is what Dean Hole the famous rose grower had to say about his funeral: "It is recorded in the *Standard* of February 11, 1892, that 'four memorial services were held at the Metropolitan Tabernacle on the day preceding, each attended by 5,500 persons. At each service all eyes were centred upon the grouping of coffin and bending palms, of white lilies, ferns, and myrtles with hanging drapery, bearing texts or words spoken by the deceased, and the white bust in the centre, a striking likeness of the late pastor.'"

He notices the same paper the next day paid more reference to the occasion. "The public pulse is getting into the habit of being at fever heat; and unless the popular humour soon changes, men really great and eminent will shrink from the humiliation of public honours, whether in life or posthumously. The exaggerated demonstrations held at the obsequies of those who have had their little day will compel the surviving kindred of really great citizens to ask to be left alone with their sorrow, and to insist on a quiet interment in some country churchyard."

I write of this because we had a similar funeral in our district which happened on my way to school. It was of the Baptist minister of the Tabernacle, Penge. I and one or two others arrived at the house just in time to see the masses of flowers being brought out, and were late in consequence. I think we were forgiven. His name was John Wesley Bowd and he came from mother's Suffolk, Earl Soham, Wickham Market. He was indeed a good man and must have begun life as a Methodist.

I have wandered a long way from our lamplit streets, because when we went to mother's home they had none at all, and the darkness was indeed overwhelming; but they were used to it. I have read somewhere that whenever the subject of lighting was broached, the old folks scorned the idea. "I can't see wot they wants the place lit up o'nights. We ha' done wi'out it all these here years an' ain't none the wus for't!" "Ah," said another, "thare's light enuf fur anybody, if they wur tew go tew bed at the proper time, an' git up arly in t' morn." Yet a third clinched the matter: "Well, they may say this an' thet, an' t'other, but I knows if they wer tew come hare an ketch a howd o' this ere scythe, an' swing thet about, from six in the morn tew five and six o'clock o' nights, they'd be whooly glad tew git tew bed."

I didn't know much about the darkness of those dear dead days in Suffolk, because I was soon in a feather bed on the floor of that little apple chamber, mine for the time being. Having been examined for flea bites before that. I must say they took full advantage of my little white limbs.

But what a place Suffolk was to me, who lived in a suburb that only arose out from nothing in the middle years of Victoria's reign. The solemnity of the years gripped me, in church and churchyard. When I grew older and could take the sacrament, I thought with what joy I could stand beneath that eastern window, with the memories and monuments of the years that were gone all about me.

I have been reading once again that lovely book by Percy Lubbock, writing of his boyhood visits and memories of his beautiful old grandmother at Earlham. He found it to be a liberal education and remarks on the appealing romance of the Norfolk names, such as Hindringham, Walsingham, Burlingham; and catches again the magic of Wramplingham. I could do much the same with those of Suffolk; Saxmundham, Snape, Eastbridge, Theberton, Framlingham, Bungay and Beccles. What wonders do they hold in those ancient bits of old England.

I do not know why my mother went to her Suffolk home to have her first baby. True, there were no such things as baby clinics in those now far-off days, and there was not much in the way of medical attention even in a London suburb; it was a case of hit or miss. In the country villages there was always one of those wise old women, who seemed more efficient than the local doctor; so mother must have placed herself in her care.

They were the sort of person to be consulted if a child was a bit off colour: "I'm a'most sure as ow he's a sickenin' for summat." To be told after a good look. "E's gort the measles right a' nuff. I ken see the spots under the skin; look yew hare! Yew giv' him a posset an' keep him a-bed, or by the fire in the warm, p'raps the rash 'ull be out come the mornin'." And they were marvellous at a bit of description when summing up a case of jaundice: "he's as yaller as a kite's foot!"

They were wonderful, too, those old grannies who had brought up a family and knew when the brick oven was right for the baking, and the beer at blood heat to put in the yeast. They might have sunken eyes and absolutely toothless mouths.

In any case the home, if it was well kept, had a store of homely medicines, such as salts and senna, brimstone and treacle. They knew the value of herbs and hedgerow plants, stewed groundsel for poultices, marsh-mallow leaves and flowers made into ointment for boils, lily leaves for cuts, dock leaves for galled feet, green broom for kidney trouble, and dandelion roots for the liver, colts' foot leaves for bronchitis and asthma, rue pills for a tonic, leaves of camomile for herb tea – this being drunk for general health.

The ladies at the rectory might have lashings of cough mixture made up to their prescription.

The wayside verges were then untouched by scythe or flashing hook, and were studded with numerous, and often rare, wild flowers. There was eye bright and the sulphur clover, even the grass vetch. And on the sides of the old ditches might be found the golden saxifrage and the white teasle.

Coming back to my mother, she was attended by a retired surgeon-major when I came into the world, and as she had lost two children in between, she became very possessive. I think the old army doctor opened his mouth a bit too wide and she soon showed her disapproval; as she did when the butcher's boy made advances when she was in her first job in London.

As for my family, when they came along, they each in turn went on a feeding course to "Black Lake", in Surrey, one of Barrie's homes where he wrote one of his plays.

4

The Felixstowe That Was

The world's a scene of changes, and to be
Constant in Nature were inconstancy,
Cowley

It is incredible to think that the rustic scene of plate 3 is within the memory of some still living in Felixstowe, and they not antiquities by any means. One can even remember playing in the old farmyard. Yet the rural atmosphere of our town has completely disappeared and we have said farewell to village life to become suburbanized, with a rate roll that would have 'whooly stammed' the old people, as my Suffolk grandfather would have exclaimed.

But that farmhouse is still there and that dusty road has become a high road, which is better described as a race track. Even that plane tree on the left is still there, now spreading its green shade on the path, and nearby is a derelict bus shelter left by the vandals. The gable end you can see in the distance is that of the old Pig and Whistle, still thatched, and now part of Felixstowe College. Naturally the farmhouse has been altered, and it is not the slightest use to go to the back door for a can of milk or a pound of Suffolk butter.

However, being by nature rather cold and probably going to depart this life by the new disease of hypothermia, I must confess to a great liking for chimneys and chimney pots. Alas, some of those of the picture have gone and we have advanced into an age when chimney pots are redundant. But how delightfully and homely do they appear as they break the outline of the scene, suggesting warmth and hospitality.

This fine old farmhouse (there are really two) dating from the sixteenth century, with an ecclesiastical background, has been converted into two distinctive residences; that splendid sweep of roof has lost something of its outline, and a high fence has taken the place of those iron rails and that open vista. It is a wonder the whole prospect was not swept away when they laid tramlines along that old highway to build Brackenbury Fort in the First World War. Truth to tell that also has disappeared.

That change is not confined to Felixstowe is evident in every morning paper. Merely a paragraph announces it, such as appeared recently in the *Daily Telegraph:* "Builders start work today on a £35,000 project to convert a 200-year-old pig-sty at Elm Farm, Horsham St Faith, Norfolk, into six holiday chalets. The pigs moved out last week. . . . The farmer said 'There's more money in people than in pigs'." Let's 'hoop' the occupants don't develop into a lot o' them owd road hogs.

In an old directory of Felixstowe dated 1901 Priory Farm had two occupants – G. Thurlow and G. Carr. I wonder if that stirs any memories?

In the old days civilization ended at Priory Farm, at least that is the suggestion given in Lacy's directory, because it states clearly: "High Road from Garrison Lane to May Bush corner, although it includes Priory Farm, which is just beyond". And you would not meet with any other life until you reached East End Farm which is now the Golf House. And thus to that haunt of individuality known as Bawdsey Ferry. There the world ends.

However, here is part of a letter written by Edward FitzGerald to W. B. Donne about 1863:

My dear Donne,

I only had your Note and its Enclosure after returning from Bawdsey Ferry (the Mouth of our Harbour) after a stay there of ten days. Thither I went because my Hostess was unwell: the Maid sent home; and I had lent my Ship (like a Fool) to the as great Fool who borrowed her 5 days to go to Holland and return in; which, 5 days spread into a fortnight, from a fierce West wind that blocked them up in the Meuse as fast as Agamemnon was at Aulis. . . .

I think you would like this Bawdsey (though the Name should hardly be mentioned to Ears polite): only about a dozen Fishermen's Houses, built where our River runs into the Sea over a foaming Bar: on one side of which is a good sand to Felixstowe and on the other an orange-coloured Crag Cliff towards Orford Haven: not a single respectable house, or Inhabitant, or Lodger: no white Cravats; an Inn with scarce Table or Chair: only Bread and Cheese to eat. I often lie there in my Boat: I wish you would come and do so.*

Just one more little touch about FitzGerald. Bernard Barton writing to William Bodham Donne from Woodbridge on 23rd March 1845:

My dear Friend,

Edward [FitzGerald] continues at the cottage. The day before yesterday being a fine Good Friday, I waded through two miles of mist and melted snow to get at him, and finding him luckily at home at half-past twelve stopt with him till just past six in the evening. He called a council with his old Dame of the Cottage, at which I assisted, as to what could be done on such an emergency about dinner, and we fared superbly – boiled salt fish and egg sauce, with a roast duck. Edward, being orthodox, stuck to the salt fish, I, more lax, attacking the wild fowl. The day passed pleasantly enough. . . .

I fear we shall hardly keep our pleasant neighbour much longer in this vicinity. He is a vast acquisition to me as an occasional dropper in – as poor Lamb was to say, "The sky does not drop such larks every day".

Thine B. B.

Returning to the Priory Farm. In the *East Anglian Notes and Queries* for 1909–10 is an account of the "Singular Circumstances Attending the Loan of a Cart by the Prior of Felixstowe,

* FitzGerald loved capital letters and the punctuation is his.

Suffolk, temp Henry VIII". It is a curiously worded document respecting the forfeiture of goods to the king (on what grounds we know not), and a subsequent change of purpose with its consequences. It is rather too long to quote in full and I have taken the liberty of modernizing the language. In short it concerns a distraint on the goods of one William Pigott of Felixstowe, the subsequent revoking of the order; and Master Pigott, with the connivance of the Sheriff, Sir Edward Jenny, walking off with cattle belonging to the prior and others.

To the King Our Soverign Lord,

In most humble wise showeth and complaineth unto your most noble grace your poor Chaplain and daily Orator [not the Park Lane type, but a spiritual advocate], Dan William Waterforde, prior of the house or cell of Filchestowe in your county of Suffolk. That whereas your highness gave unto your poor subject Richard Cawndisshe, Esq. all the goods of one William Pigott of Filchestowe aforesaid . . . whereupon the said Cawndisshe prayed and required your said orator to lend him his cart to convey away the goods according to your said gift. And because your said orator lent unto the said Cawndisshe, his cart, and for no other reason the said Pigott with the aid and comfort of Sir Edmund Jenny, attached as well divers cattle of your said orator, as of other persons and then took and conveyed them away at their pleasure. And so the same keepeth and witholdest them from your orator against all right and conscience and over that duly vexeth and troubleth the same your orator so that he cannot serve God as he would do. Therefore please it Your Highness . . . to direct your gracious letters under your privy signet . . . to make deliverance of all the said cattle unto your orator and also to suffice him peaceably to dwell and abide without any vexation or trouble in any wise. And he shall during his life pray to God for the preservation of your most excellent and Royal estate.

We are not told of the sequel if there was one. However, one wonders what sort of cart it was, what it was normally used for and whence the goods and cattle were conveyed. Remembering the only way out of old Felixstowe was through the dust track of

Walton. Evidently the poor prior was a farmer as well as a priest, probably running this same old Priory Farm. The said William Pigott must have cocked a snook at the poor man as he departed, using somebody else's cart, probably drawn by bullocks – hence the theft of cattle.

To speak of the change in Felixstowe, since this picture was taken and sold in one of the fancy shops that then existed in our main street, as being phenomenal is to put it very mildly. There were farms almost at our door. Our own road was not made up and cows grazed in a field at our end of the road. The farmer would come daily to call them home and the leader would take her place. As soon as they touched hard ground would let loose their pats.

Cornfields were just behind the houses opposite, so we not only had a harvest moon, to remind us that harvest men did not strike work when the sun went down but, as we face the sea, a fisherman's moon also, making a pathway across the water. It would be difficult to drive home a herd of cows today past what was the old Priory Farm.

Besides that the place was full of individual characters bearing local names that still exist, happily, such as Andrews, Bloomfield, Cordy, Durrant, Everett; one of whom was a saddler and harness maker. Milk was still delivered by a horse-drawn float, and a local baker of very pleasant mien called at our door with a basket of bread on his arm for us to choose from. Newson was, and still is, a well-known name at the Ferry; you can see the names lined up in our old churchyard – "Drowned at Sea". One wonders too, how many other drowned sailors, washed up on our beach, lie in our churchyard with no known grave.

Two advertisements speak for themselves of not so crowded a population or so urbanized a little east-coast seaside town, with a prize-winning railway station. For instance W. H. Cordy, Baker, Confectioner and Dairyman, advertised that at their restaurant they catered for schools and choir outings. And this: "Established over a quarter of a century [in 1910] J. Smith,

Pork Butcher and Poulterer, High Street Walton. Try our Noted Sausages. Last year's sales, 18,788 lb. Home-cured hams and bacon, home-tried lard. All orders by post receive personal attention. Delivery to all parts daily."

They used to call on us once a week with sausages and eggs, the former made to a special recipe of an old granny of the family. Then one day they called for the last time, having sold the business to a local purveyor, which, of course, soon passed out of our ken.

We arrived too late to meet the Emenys, who captured for as long as Felixstowe will last, their times and seasons. They have left a great record for those who enjoy local history, and they are many. Needless to say this rapid change has come about by the Felixstowe docks, with their sea-link of so wide a compass.

However, with it all, although we can no longer hear the harvesters at work, we have not far to seek a field of pure gold, shimmering in the sun, producing a crop of rape seed. Surely it is a reminder that we were, and still are, dependent upon our earth for its increase.

When the cornfields opposite to us, incidentally the most historic part of the village, were turned into a housing estate, a man operating a mechanical digger in working a deep trench, turned up one of the most beautiful flint sickles I have ever seen. So we were farmers and tillers of the fields even before the Romans came. We may be indeed proud of our past, since the old priory was the first building to appear in Filchestowe after the Norman castle, thus linking us with the outside world of long ago at Rochester in Kent, and thereby to heaven.

5

Matthew Parker

Mild monastic faces in quiet collegiate cloisters.
Arthur Clough

That Suffolk never lagged behind in cooking and feasting might be exemplified by Matthew Parker, a Norwich man, who was to become the seventieth Archbishop of Canterbury. (His father, a tradesman, was a callenderer of stuff.) In the reign of Henry VIII he held the office of chaplain to the Queen and later to the King, and thereby was assigned the deanery of Stoke-by-Clare in 1538, which was pleasantly situated in a close surrounded by six acres of land and an orchard. It was richly endowed with lands, rents, tithes, portions and pensions in fifty-six parishes. Among the endowments was the payments of 8,000 eels annually from Fordiam and Lackenheath.

For some twelve or thirteen years this was Parker's happy home. Here he delighted to gather his friends around him, a place which seemed, as it were, created for scholars both to receive and impart instruction. An occasional supply of venison from the royal forests enabled him to entertain his neighbours.

While at Stoke, his larder was frequently supplied by the kind consideration of the Queen Consort and, with a command of eels at all times he found no difficulty in keeping up this hospitality, which implied the providing board at a common table to all who lodged within the precincts of the college. Into his garden he introduced the tuber-rose and the pink, and regaled his friends occasionally with apricots, which had been lately introduced from Epirus.

Matthew was a young man, in his early thirties, having been ordained priest in 1527. I wonder what the old house was like which fascinated him so much? Rambling old rooms with more than four sides to them, into which one had to step down, or even up, so you would need a rushlight in the dark corners; and doors galore, that seemed to hold old memories, and little leaded-light windows that, when the cobwebs were cleared away, looked out into little gardens full of old-fashioned flowers. A place that cast a spell on one, delightful when the sun shone, casting long beams on the wide planks of the uneven floor, but a bit ominous when the shadows fell. Some of the rooms completely forgotten, so that if you made a tour you would wonder where they led to, and if anyone had ever used them. But on the whole a great place in which a scholar might work; and Matthew Parker was that. And he lived here before he was married.

There were two places here that were full of life especially when Parker was a resident. One was the great hall, where he dined with his friends and neighbours, and the other was the kitchen.

In the latter was the great open fireplace, where hung soot-covered pots by means of hooks, and presumably in the chimney would be hams and sides of animals awaiting their turn. Before the fire would be the spit on which the great joints of venison would be basting, tended by a cook with a basting ladle. Under this was what was known in Suffolk as the latchpan to catch the gravy that was constantly being poured back over the roasting meat.

There would be a huge table in the middle of the room, made there with huge planks wide enough and heavy enough to make timbers for a ship. This would be covered with pans for cleaning the vegetables and preparing the frills for the feast. The tankards of ale would be brought in from the brewing house. No wonder Matthew was sad when he was ousted from this, to him, so happy a home.

Presumably when at the college he would have attended the church now known as St John. I was interested to note that the register dates from 1538, whilst Parker was there. Today, there is a little of the fifteenth-century glass in the transept window, showing a windmill, and in a quarry a white hart, so the emphasis was on venison, and Matthew may have glanced on these details when he was there. One of its chief treasures is a beautiful fifteenth-century pulpit that is only 28 ins wide, so it would only hold an ascetic; and the medieval clock bell is inscribed: "Rise in the morning to serve God".

When he became archbishop it fell to his lot to pass judgement on Lady Katherine Grey although he acted only as a member of a commission. She, as a maid of honour to the imperious and suspicious Elizabeth I, had contracted a marriage with the Earl of Hertford, and had given birth to a son. It was thought at the time that the marriage had never taken place, and it was much later that a priest came forward and stated he had performed it. This issue, to Elizabeth's horror, came in direct line with the throne, Katherine being sister to the unfortunate Queen Jane; and Elizabeth feared there might be a plot.

Both Lady Katherine and Lord Hertford were sent to the Tower on 5th September 1562. On 10th February 1563 Lady Hertford had another son, and Machyn in his diary says: "The godfathers were two warders of the Tower; and his name was called Thomas". The elder boy was named Edward.

The confinement was not very strict, and although state prisoners were not allowed to go beyond the precincts of the Tower, these were extensive. Lady Katherine was, during part of the time, lodged within the Tower itself; but she was permitted to receive visits from her friends. Being of royal birth, she was treated with respect due to her rank, so far as this was consistent with her safe keeping. There is still a list extant of the furniture provided by the government for her convenience. It consisted of "five pieces of tapestry to hang the chamber; three window pieces of the like stuff; a sparver for the bed of changeable silk damask; a silk quilt of red striped gold; a bed and a bolster of down, with two pillows of down; one white linen quilt stuffed with wool; four pairs of fustians, the one of six breadths and the other of five; two carpets of Turkey making, one small window carpet; one chair of cloth of gold raised with crimson velvets, with two points of copper gilt, and the queen's arms on the back; one cushion of purple velvet; two footstools covered with green velvet; one cupboard joined; and one bed and bolster, and a counterpane for the woman".

Sir Edward Warner depreciated the furniture as old and dilapidated; but then he would claim it as his perquisite on the release of the prisoners. And while he would complain if the best of all things were not provided, the government knowing that it was doubtful how long the prisoners would remain in his custody, would not want to be put to more expense than possible. The dignity, not the comfort, of the prisoners was consulted. In a letter to Sir William Cecil in September 1563, Sir Edward attributed the injury done to the furniture by the gambols of the Lady Katherine's monkeys and dogs.

So much care was taken of Lady Katherine that, when the plague broke out in 1563, she was immediately sent to the home of her uncle, Lord John Grey at Pyrgo in Essex. According to the custom of the time, she was his prisoner and he was responsible for her safe keeping.

In 1565, the Lady Katherine and her husband were recommitted to the Tower under the charge of Sir Owen Hopton. The Queen directed him to take into his charge the Lady Katherine Grey, but to keep her from access of all strangers. Her health failing she was permitted occasionally, for the sake of change of air, to be removed to Yoxford, where she died at Cockfield Hall, on 27th January in the tenth year of Queen Elizabeth's reign.

Going back to Matthew Parker – after he was ousted from Clare he was made Dean of Lincoln. In 1547 he married Margaret Harleston, daughter of Robert Harleston in the county of Norfolk – a lady by birth and manners. He was forty-two and she twenty-eight. It was said never was man more fortunate.

Mrs Parker, according to the custom of the age had received an education which enabled her to sympathize with her husband in his station and ecclesiastical pursuits; at the same time she was endowed with such sound common sense, that she managed his household affairs as to enable him to keep hospitality without being involved in debt.

Although Parker was somewhat timid and would never have made a martyr himself, as was shown when he visited Kett's rebellion at Norwich, he accompanied Thomas Bilney, "little of stature and very slender of body" to his death at Hadleigh. He was deprived of all his preferments under Mary Tudor and went into retirement. He was a great student, made a metrical version of the Psalms and took the lead in liturgical reform. For the Bishops' Bible he translated the Books of Genesis and Exodus in the Old Testament; and in the New, St Matthew's and St Mark's Gospels, with the Epistles of St Paul, excepting the Epistle to the Romans and the First to the Corinthians. He was responsible also for the Thirty-nine Articles reducing them from Forty-two, and for the Calendar of the Saints.

He was created Archbishop of Canterbury in 1559, the second of the reforming bishops, but he was never a wholehearted Protestant. His wife died before him and, like many of his predecessors, he prepared his own tomb which was of black marble and also wrote the inscription for his own monument. He was accustomed to go there often to meditate. He died on 17th May 1575.

The Puritans, who hated Parker, stigmatizing him as the pope of Lambeth, pursued him long after his death. In the reign of Charles I they tore down his monument, broke open his tomb, exhumed his body and cast it on a dung hill. Curiously enough, his bones were rescued by the Suffolk-born Archbishop Sancroft and re-interred in the reign of James I.

Stoke College is still there, now a private school. The house is described as Queen Anne, so that cannot be the one Matthew Parker so much loved. But there is a red Tudor dovecote with portcullis, that stands beside the entrance. It must have been there when Matthew walked in and out.

I have sometimes wondered why Plantagenet and Tudor monarchs when bestowing their favours often requested part of their payment should be in eels (it was herrings at Dunwich). This may be explained by a letter which appeared in *Country Life* in 1900 by the Rev. C. J. Cornish, who was vicar of Debenham over a century ago:

> The way in which eels manage to maintain themselves in every kind of water is surprising. There is no pond so small or muddy, or brook so insignificant, that eels are not found in it. If the pool dries up, they either bury themselves in the mud or make their way over the dewy grass by night, like snakes, to some other water. You never find an eel left high and dry, as you do roach and carp in field ponds in hot summers. Their migration to the sea to breed is evidence of their extreme vitality, though it is probable that when the eel once does breed it dies. That is the experience of the Marine Biological Labority in Plymouth, where the congers have been kept and have deposited their eggs. The hardiness and fecundity of eels, shown by their power to live out of water, and the million of elvers coming up the large rivers at 'eel-fare' season, are among the few cases in which a really valuable and high-priced natural article is made plentiful. As an instance of the number and returns given by eels I may quote the following: "At a mill on a small Sussex river two eel cages are set during the winter. The miller expects to catch in one night 5 cwt of eels." This seems an incredible quantity, but I find on reliable authority that it is true.

6

The Passing of Lady Katherine Grey

Now thus but like to change
And fade as do the the flowre
Which springe and bloom full gay,
And wythrethe in one hour.

The importance and station of the Lady Katherine Grey was that she was the great-granddaughter of Henry VII, through his daughter Mary Tudor, for so short a time Queen of France. Queen Elizabeth had no heir while Katherine had issue as we have seen. She was near the throne more than once, especially when Elizabeth was ill at Hampton Court and near death when suffering from small-pox aggravated by a chill.

The clandestine marriage of Lady Katherine is of considerable interest, showing how young women in high places could act as schemers, or love would find a way. When she became betrothed to Lord Hertford, she said: "Weighing your loving suit and great good-will towards me, I am well content, be the consequences what they may, to marry you the next time the Queen's Highness shall go abroad and leave the Lady Jane (Seymour) alone with me."

Some five or six days afterwards Queen Elizabeth decided to go with her train to Greenwich on a hunting expedition, and summoned her ladies to accompany her. Lady Katherine excused herself on the plea that she had a bad attack of toothache and exhibited a swollen face tied up in a kerchief; whilst Lady Jane Seymour said she had a bad headache. The Queen accepted these excuses.

Scarcely had she gone when the young ladies stole out from the palace, and went to Hertford's house in Cannon Row, Westminster. There a priest was waiting and the marriage took place. But they had been seen by Powell the cook.

During the plague in London, Katherine was sent to Pyrgo, as already stated. This was near Havering-atte-Bower and Hainault Forest in Essex, the gardens of which were very fine, but her captor was very cruel. When he died she was sent to Ingatestone House and afterwards to Gosfield, near Halstead, Essex. A letter from the Queen, dated Windsor, 2nd October 1567, commanded Sir Owen Hopton to convey the Lady Katherine and her train, to his house, Cockfield Hall, in Yoxford, some thirty miles distant.

The party spent a night en route at Ipswich, the landlord's bill is among the State Papers:

> Imprimis; expended at Ipswich upon the receipt of the Lady Katherine for one supper and one dinner, fire, lodging and horsemeat there £7 15s.
>
> Item; for one bait at Snape when the Lady Katherine came from Ipswich to Cockfield, 20s.
>
> Item; for the hire of a cart for the carriage of the stuff and apparel of the same Lady Katherine from Ipswich to Cockfield, 20s.
>
> Item; given in reward for the coach, 10s.

Soon after her arrival at Yoxford she became very ill and Sir Owen sent for Dr Symonds, the Queen's physician who duly visited her. After his departure she became worse and he paid a second visit at Hopton's behest, who exclaimed: "He then shall show his cunning and God shall do the cure". But Lady Katherine knew that she was dying and asked for the passing bell to be tolled, which was done.

A document still survives, *The Manner of Her Departing*. She repeated portions of the Book of Common Prayer and asked for her jewel box. Taking from it a ring with a pointed diamond, she asked for it to be returned to Lord Hertford. Sir Owen asked if it was her wedding ring? "No," she replied, "that was the ring of my assurance [betrothal], there is my wedding ring," requesting that it should go to her husband also. Then she took out another inscribed: "While I live yours", saying, "This shall be the last token to my Lord that ever I shall send him; it is the picture of myself." After this it was noticed that her nails were turning purple, and she exclaimed: "Lo, He comes! Yea, even so come Lord Jesus!" She died at nine o'clock in the morning of the 27th January 1568, aged twenty-seven.

Her body was evidently embalmed as the following expenses appear: "Itm; for one Mr Hannse S'geon, for cering the corpse £3. Itm; for spice, flax, rosin, wax, and the coffin making and for the serge clothes, £3." The funeral took place on 21st February 1568 in Yoxford church, in the presence of seventy-seven mourners, but nobody of great note attended. Hertford was not allowed to be present, even by proxy. There was only a meagre display of banners etc, usual at state and semi-state funerals, but there is indication that the service was choral. A sum of £4 17s. 8d. was dispersed to the poor after the funeral. A list of the items of expenditure made up by Sir Owen Hopton, is of considerable interest:

Item; for sending to London three times while the Lady Katherine was sick, £35.

Itm; for the charge of Doctor Simondes and his man and his horse at Cockfield twice [left blank].

Itm; for my own charge two times coming to London [also blank].

Imprimis; for four meals and two nights' lodging of all the mourners, being to the number of 77, for their horsemeat during the time, £40. Besides a great number of comers to see the solemnity of that burial.

Itm; paid to the singing men at the same funeral, 20s.
Itm; paid for the watchers of the Lady Katherine, 40s.

Then follow the heralds' fees.

For the liveries of one herald, 5 yards at 16s. the yard, £4.

For the herald's fee, £3 6s. 8d., and for his transportation hither and back again at 6d. a mile, £3 7s.

For Mr Garter's fee, £10.

To the painter, for a great banner of arms, 50s.

For 6 great scutcheons of paper in metal for garnishing of the house and the church, and 6 dozen of paper scutcheons in colours, £6 8s.

'Itm; paid to the tailors for working of the cloth & other things upon the hearse, 20s.

By a warrant to the Exchequer of 10th March 1568, Hopton received £140 "for the board of our cousin the Lady Katherine and of her servants while she was in his keeping, and for charges for her coming thither, as also for money laid out by him in household charges during her sickness and belonging thereunto".

What great days those must have been in the peaceful Suffolk village of Yoxford where my grandmother was born. I wonder if faint echoes of that pomp and circumstance event lingered on to her days? And who were those singing men? Surely not from out the local quire? But it is all too far away and long ago to ask these questions. Yet the Lady Katherine's room is still to be found at Cockfield Hall, although her body went to rest beside her husband's in an elaborate tomb at Salisbury Cathedral, the young and handsome man she loved so much when she was a laughing and carefree maiden. Meanwhile the history of our England has added many pages to its story, and the Spanish intriguers lost their power in the great Armada.

1 & 2 Items from a village shop, from Middleton Old Post Office

3 Priory Farm

4 The corner of Cage Lane, Walton, Felixstowe, with the founder of Smith's Pork Butcher, alias Swacher Smith

7

Frumenty

Old Pot, good soup.

Although my mother and aunt, born in the 'fifties of last century, used to delight on the memories of frumenty or frummety, I had no idea of its antiquity and widespread enjoyment. It seems to have been known and prepared all over England. Moreover, it appears to have been the oldest dish that had survived the ages. It formed part of the royal banquet of Henry IV at Winchester, and at the coronation feast of Henry VII. It was eaten in the twelve days of Christmas, 25th December to 5th January, and was also a dish for Mothering Sunday.

Major Moor in his *Suffolk Vocabulary* (1823), speaks thus of it: "Frumenty – wheat boiled in milk, with cinnamon and sugar; an excellent thing". A saying recommending foresight runs thus: "When ta rain frumenty mind ye heent a dish to seek". It is readily derived from frumentation.

"Frumenty," saith old Cocker, "is broth of milk and wheat; the chief entertainment on St Luke's day at Horn Fair, kept at Charlton, near Greenwich." Although Horn Fair is still continued with undiminished festivity, frumenty is not, unhappily, among the good things which now continue thereto.

Tusser knew of the good thing, and calls it Furmenty:

> Remember thou therefore, though I do not,
> The Seed cake, the pasties, and furmenty pot.

In a supplement to Forby's *Vocabulary*, frumenty is just mentioned: "a potage made of boiled wheat; a frumentation".

It is mentioned in the 1551 Bible: "And ye shall eat neither bread, nor parched corn, nor frumenty of new corne, until the selfsame days that ye have brought an offering unto your God." Leviticus 23:14. (This was also known as the Bug Bible, because of its translation of Psalm 91:5, which reads "afraid of the bug by night", instead of the "terror by night".

Frumenty had to be prepared overnight with what was known as creed wheat, *i.e.* wheat soaked in water for twelve hours and boiled for two. In the poorer homes it was made from wheat gathered by gleaning in the fields after harvest and stored up for Christmas. It was customary in Yorkshire for the baker to have special days for 'creeing' wheat for frumenty. If gleaned the first job was to remove the husks. According to my mother this was done by placing the wheat in a sack and she and her brother swung it from end to end with much glee.

Here follows a Suffolk recipe with a delightful ending: "Frumenty wheat one quart, milk one quart, stoned raisins two tablespoonfuls; sugar to sweeten, a little nutmeg. About 10 to 15 minutes to boil up the cree'd wheat with the milk. And some was placed on a plate outside the door at night for the Pharisees [fairies]."

How was it that it died out so completely and utterly? One writer says it lasted until the First World War, but I think it was long before that. If you ask anyone born towards the closing years of last century, and of country origin, all they can say is, I have heard my father and mother talk about it but I have never had any. Was it when gleaning in the fields ended?

The late E. R. Cooper, giving a lecture on "Farmhouse Life Fifty years Ago" in 1933, said this:

> Furmenty, or frumenty, was a very old Suffolk dish made from whole wheat; I cannot find the exact recipe but believe the wheat was first wetted and stood by the fire to soften and swell, that it was then boiled in milk, sweetened with sugar and flavoured with

cinnamon. I never tasted any, but often heard it well spoken of.

At Sunday School my mother once asked a girl what God made on the second day of the Creation, she replied: "Please ma'am He made some furmetty."

Here follows some recipes, gathered by Florence White, founder of the English Folk Cooking Association, and published in 1932, in which one can note the strong similarity.

A good one comes from Staffordshire:

1. To prepare the unhusked wheat.

Take good white new wheat; just wet it a little; put it in a coarse bag and beat it with a stick until the external husk is loose enough to be rubbed off; wash it well, change the water 5 or 6 times till free from the bran; put it in a stewpot with plenty of water; cover it and set it in an oven (on a red tile) until the wheat is quite soft; when cold it will be a jelly with the burst cooked grains of wheat in it. This is known as cree'd wheat or frumenty wheat.

2. To prepare cree'd or frumenty wheat for the table.

Put as much as is required into a pan with sufficient milk, stirring constantly with a wooden spoon. When nearly boiling add a small quantity of flour mixed smooth with milk, adding sugar, grated nutmeg, cinnamon, lemon peel, pimento (sweet pepper) or a bay leaf for flavouring, or you can thicken the frumenty with yolks of eggs mixed with a little milk (beaten well) or the whole of the eggs – this is used instead of flour for thickening. Currants and sultanas can be added, but the fruit must first be boiled separately to the point of bursting, and then be added to the frumenty and cooked with it for a short time.

Frumenty. To a quarter of a pint of wheat, that has been boiled tender in milk, but not pulped, add a quart of new milk or cream, a piece of cinnamon, equal quantities of sugar and well washed currants, three ounces of each, and boil for fifteen minutes longer. Take the mixture off the fire and stir in (if only milk is used) the beaten yolks of three eggs and a glass of brandy; send to table in a junket bowl, to be served in cups. Time to boil wheat from three to four hours.

Frumenty (another way). To one quart of ready boiled wheat allow two quarts of new milk; keep the whole stirred over a slow fire, and from time to time, throw in well washed currants and stoned raisins, allowing about a quarter of a pound of the fruit to the above quantity of milk. When sufficiently boiled, remove from the fire and stir in the beaten yolks of three eggs, previously mixed with a little milk. Flavour with nutmeg, cinnamon, and sweeten to taste. Do not boil again, but stir for a few minutes over the fire. It is sometimes served in cups, with brandy as an additional flavouring. Time to boil wheat three to four hours; to simmer with milk, twenty minutes. (Cassels *Dictionary of Cooking* (1881).)

Lincolnshire Frumenty. Ingredients: Frumenty wheat, 1 quart: milk 1 quart; stoned raisins a tablespoonful; sugar to sweeten, a little nutmeg.

Time: about 10 to 15 minutes to boil up the cree'd wheat with the milk.

Put the cree'd wheat and milk on together and boil up. When it begins to thicken add some allspice, or (as some call it) sweet pepper, which can be bought at either the grocer's or chemist's. Finally make a little flour into a thin cream with a little cold milk and stir it into the frumenty; boil up and serve.

To make Furmety (1821):

Take wheat and wet it, then beat it in a sack with a Wash Beetle. Being finely hulled and cleansed, boil it overnight and let it soak on a soft fire all night. Then next morning take as much as will serve the turn, put it in a Pipkin, Pan, or Skillet, and put it a boiling in cream or milk, mace, salt, cinnamon, saffron or yolks of eggs. Boil it thick and serve it in a clean scoured dish, scrape of sugar and trim the Dish.

8

Some Suffolk Cooking

Digestion is the business of the Stomach and indigestion that of the doctors. 1758.

Suffolk produced at least two cookery experts. One was Mary Easton of Bungay, 1823, and the other Eliza Acton, born at Ipswich, 1799. Her *Modern Cooking* was published in 1845. Some of their recipes were collected by Florence White and published in her *Good Things in England* (1932) by Jonathan Cape.

So we might proceed with a few of their recipes with the words of Eliza Acton in our ears: "Roasting which is quite a favourite mode of dressing meat in this country, and one in which the English are said to excel, requires unremitting attention on the part of the cook rather than any great exertion of skill." But to start with we must have the "*Cook's Herb Patch*: chives, parsley, sage, thyme, mint, fennel, winter savoury, sweet marjoram, sweet basil and tarragon."

We will take Mary Easton first.

Vegetable Water Soup. Ingredients: cabbage ¼; carrots 4; parsnips 2; onions 6; turnips 3; celery root 1; parsley root, a small one; white beet leaves and chervil; peas ½ pint tied up in a piece of linen.

Wash the vegetables but do not cut them up. Put them in a saucepan holding about 2 quarts. Add water to fill the saucepan 3 parts full. Stew for 3 hours. Strain off the broth and return it to the saucepan. Add some salt. Cut up some of the vegetables into dice with the peas, and use all these to garnish the soup. Heat and serve.

Stock for Gravy or Gravy Soup. Ingredients: lean beef 1 lb; lean gammon of bacon 1 lb; water 2 quarts; scraped carrots about 8 oz; onions 6 oz, (peeled brings about 4 oz); and scrubbed and stringy celery about 8 sticks.

Slice and cut up the meat. Slice the vegetables and add them to the meat. Stew until the meat is quite tender but do not let it brown.

The meat if only boiled until tender, will make a delicious meat loaf or potted meat for luncheon or breakfast.

Stuffing for Veal, Roast Turkey or Hare. Ingredients: bread crumbs 4 oz; finely chopped beef suet 4 oz; finely chopped parsley and sweet herbs 1 teaspoonful; salt $\frac{1}{2}$ teaspoonful; grated lemon peel, a little; raw egg or milk to bind. Pound all together and moisten with egg or milk.

Smelts. When good and in season, they have a fine silvery hue, are very firm and have a refreshing smell like cucumbers newly cut. They should not be washed more than is necessary merely to clean them. Dry them in a cloth, lightly flour them, and shake it off. Dip them in plenty of egg, then into fine bread-crumbs. Plunge them into a good pan of boiling lard. Let them continue boiling and a few minutes will make them a bright yellow brown. Take care not to take off the light roughness of the crumb, or their beauty will be lost.

Stewed Oysters. Ingredients: oysters; mace, a bit; lemon peel; pepper, a few white ones; butter and flour; cream; sippets of toast.

Open the oyster shells. Separate the liquor from the oysters. Beard them. Strain the liquor into a stewpan, add the oysters a bit of mace, lemon peel, and a few white peppers. Simmer them very gently for 5 minutes, strain, take out the lemon peel, peppers and mace, return them and the liquor to the stewpan; put in some cream; and when that is hot through, add the flour rolled into the butter. Simmer 5 minutes and serve piping hot. They may be served in the deep halves of the oyster shells, which must be thoroughly washed and scrubbed.

Spare-Rib of Pork. Baste it with a very little butter and flour. When done sprinkle with dried sage leaves crumbled. Serve with potatoes and apple sauce.

Snipe. These birds will keep several days and should be roasted without drawing, and then served on toast. Butter only should be eaten with them, as gravy takes from the fine flavour. The thigh and back are most esteemed.

Suffolk Dumplings. Ingredients: dough made with yeast and milk as for bread. Time to boil 20 minutes.

Let the dough rise one hour before the fire, Make the dough into balls the size of a middling apple. Throw them into boiling water, and let them boil 20 minutes. To ascertain when they are done enough, stick a fork into one; and if it comes out clear, they are ready to take up.

Do not cut, but tear apart on the top with two forks, for they become heavy by their own steam. They should be eaten immediately, with gravy, or cold butter, or with meat.

Strawberries in Wine. Ingredients: the finest strawberries; castor sugar; Madeira or fine sherry (or better still, a bottle of home-made orange wine). Hull the fruit and put it in a Kilner fruit-bottling jar, or any wide necked bottle. Sprinkle a very little sugar over each layer. Fill up with wine. And fasten securely.

Strawberry and Raspberry Fool. Ingredients: scarlet strawberries 1 pint; raspberries 1 pint; castor sugar $\frac{1}{2}$ lb; orange-flower water 1 tablespoonful; cream $1\frac{1}{2}$ pints; some fine strawberries for decoration. Boil 2 or 3 minutes. Bruise the strawberries and raspberries. Pass them through a hair sieve. Mix them with sugar and orange-flower water. Boil up the cream and stir it till it is cold. Beat the fruit pulp and the cold cream together. Stir them till they are well mixed. Put the fool into glasses or pile in bowls as you think fit.

Gooseberry Fool. This is made in the same way, but the gooseberries have to be stewed until they are soft enough to pulp; they should not, however, be rubbed through a sieve, because this process somewhat lessens their flavour. Just bruise them and whisk them to a smooth pulp. Now to Eliza Acton:

Ruth Pinch's Beefsteak Pudding, from *Martin Chuzzlewit.*

For a basin that holds 1½ pints of water the following quantities will be required. Ingredients: flour 1 lb; beef suet finely minced 6 oz [or if you are a Ruth Pinch 6 ozs butter]; water ½ pint (or the yolks of 4 eggs, and a little water); beefsteak 1 lb (the skirt makes an excellent pudding and is economical); salt ½ oz; pepper ½ teaspoonful; mutton may be substituted for beef, and a half a dozen oysters interspersed with it.

Grease a basin, put a large pot of water on to boil. Make the pastry with the flour, suet [or butter], salt and water (or eggs). Roll it out and line the basin leaving a piece for the lid. Cut the steak into convenient pieces, flour and season them with pepper and salt; put them in the pudding. Pour in ¼ pint of water, and put on the lid. Tie over with a floured cloth, and boil 3½ hours.

Pease Pudding (to serve with boiled pork). Ingredients: split peas 1 pint; butter 1 oz; salt, pepper. (Or butter 1½ oz; and eggs 3.)

Wash the peas, and soak them all night in plenty of cold soft water (if the water is hard half a teaspoonful of carbonate of soda must be stirred into the water in which the peas are boiled). Next day tie them up in a thick closely woven pudding cloth giving them room to swell or they will be hard, but not too much or they will be watery, and if they are it is impossible to make them into a pudding. Put them into a saucepan with cold water to well cover them, bring them to boiling point and boil them for 2 to 2½ hours. Lift them into a colander and let the water drain off, untie the cloth and crush the peas into a paste with a wooden spoon. Stir in the butter, pepper and salt, tie up very tightly and boil for half an hour (if made with eggs 1 hour). Turn the pudding very gently into a dish that it may not break, and serve it as hot as possible.

English Salad Sauce. Ingredients: hard-boiled eggs 2; salt 1 small saltspoonful; pounded sugar 1 large saltspoonful; cayenne a few grains; cold water 1 teaspoonful; sweet cream ¼ pint; chilli vinegar 1 tablespoonful; ordinary vinegar 1 tablespoonful.

The first essential for a smooth well-made English salad dressing is to have the yolks of the eggs used for it sufficiently hard to be reduced easily to a perfect paste. They should be boiled at least 15 minutes, and should have become quite cold before they are taken from the shells. They should also be well covered with water when they are cooked, or some parts of them will be tough, and will spoil the appearance of the sauce by rendering it lumpy unless they be worked through a sieve, a process which is always better avoided if possible. Mash up the hard-boiled yolks to a paste with the back of a wooden spoon. Well mix in the salt, sugar and cayenne and blend with cold water. Stir the cream in by degrees. Add the vinegar next, stirring the sauce briskly.

Potato Salad Dressing. Miss Acton called this the poet's recipe and said it was the result of great experience and reflection.

Two well-boiled potatoes passed through a sieve. A teaspoonful of mustard; 2 teaspoonfuls of salt; essence of anchovy. About ¼ teaspoonful of very finely chopped onions (well bruised) must be incorporated with this mixture. Add 3 tablespoonfuls olive oil, and 1 tablespoonful of vinegar, and the yolks of 2 hard-boiled eggs mashed to a paste. Stir up the salad immediately before dinner.

Eliza Acton's Gingerbread Biscuits. Ingredients: treacle ¾ lb; butter ½ lb; flour 1 lb; brown sugar ½ lb; ginger ¾ oz. Bake about 30 to 45 minutes.

Mix the flour with the brown sugar and the ginger. Melt the treacle and the butter together. Pour hot on to the flour mixture. Make into a paste, leave all night. When quite cold roll out thin as for biscuits with just as much flour as will prevent it sticking to the board. Cut into rounds and bake on greased and floured tins in a gentle oven.

Eliza Acton's Gingerbread, 1845.

Ingredients: eggs 5; treacle 1¼ lbs; flour 1 lb; butter 6 oz; pale brown sugar 6 oz; ground ginger 1 oz; lemons, grated rind of 2. Beat eggs well. Add warmed syrup gradually, beating all the time. Add sugar in same manner. Add butter which must be warmed but not hot. Add the ginger to the flour and sift the two together. Add to egg mixture. Beat till bubbles appear in batter, then add flavouring. Bake in greased shallow tin in slow oven.

Other Suffolk Recipes:

To Fry Sprats. A good Southwold recipe.

Wash and dry the sprats well. Dust with flour or fine oatmeal. Sprinkle the bottom of the frying pan with warm salt. Make it hot. Then put in your sprats and fry them a nice brown. No fat is needed as the salt draws out the fat of the sprats.

Suffolk sweet-cured hams. Ingredients: a leg of pork; salt of prunella 1 oz; saltpetre 1½ oz; coarse salt 1 lb; bay salt 4 oz; coarse sugar 1½ lb; treacle ½ lb. Rub the ham hard for an hour with the above ingredients well mixed. Let the ham remain in the pickle one month. Rub it as directed three times a week during the month. Then smoke it for 3 weeks.

Suffolk Cakes. Ingredients: eggs 4; fine white sugar ½ lb; lemon, the grated rind of half; butter ¼ lb; flour ¼ lb.

Beat the whites and yolks of the eggs separately; the whites to be beaten to a very stiff froth, and the well beaten yolks added. Sift in the sugar. Add the grated rind of half a lemon. Beat in the butter which must be warmed. Sift in the flour. Bake in nests of small moulds, or small separate tins.

Pork and Onion Dumpling. Ingredients: flour ¾ lb; suet 6 oz; salt ½ small teaspoonful; about 1½ gills of cold water (all this is for the crust). To fill it, pork 2 lbs; onions 1½ lbs; pepper and salt to season; water 1 gill. Grease basin. Make and roll out crust. Line basin, reserving a piece of the suet pastry to cover the top. Cut the pork into pieces, also the onions. Arrange them in the crust-lined basin in alternate layers seasoning each. When full add a gill of water. Put the crust on top. Cover with greased paper and then tie up in a pudding cloth and steam 4 or 5 hours.

Treacle Custard. A Southwold recipe well over a century old. Ingredients: short crust; egg 1; syrup 2 tablespoonfuls. Time about 30 to 40 minutes.

Grease a sandwich tin, or deep plate with the short crust. Beat up the egg. Warm the syrup so that it is liquid. Beat up the egg and the syrup together. Pour it into the pastry-lined tin or plate. Bake in a slow oven till a golden brown. Eat cold, when the mixture will set like a jelly.

Sir Charles Rowley's Plum Pudding, 1857. Ingredients: raisins ½ lb; good beef suet ½ lb; flour 7 oz; sugar 2 oz; eggs 2; a little salt. Cut the suet very large. Mix the dry ingredients together. Bind with the eggs well beaten. Put in a cloth wrung out of hot water and floured. Boil 5 hours.

General Forbes's Ginger Beer, 1857. Ingredients: Water 3½ gallons; bruised ginger 3 oz; lemons 2; loaf sugar 3 lb; cream of tartar 1 oz; yeast 2 tablespoonfuls (or 1 oz compressed yeast); 1 egg white. Time ½ hour to boil, 2 nights to stand.

Bruise the ginger and boil it for ½ hour in water. Wash the lemons and slice them and put them in a pan. Add the cream of tartar and the sugar broken up. Strain the ginger-flavoured water over the lemons. When lukewarm (i.e. fermented) with the yeast put on a piece of toast. Let it stand 2 nights. Take off the scum. Whisk the white of an egg in the ginger beer before bottling it.

God's Kitchel: A cake given to godchildren at their asking a blessing. The last place in Suffolk to sell these was at Aldeburgh.

I don't know if any of these old recipes appeal to my readers, but I think there must be one or two. Perhaps I am not a good judge as I am a lover of puddings. The spare-rib of pork makes my mouth water, especially the crackling. Pork in those days was something to be reckoned with, and almost melted in the mouth. Before sitting down to this I would suggest, as a sort of grace before meat, Lamb's "Dissertation Upon Roast Pig".

Do you remember it? How Bo-bo the errant boy inadvertently set alight to his home in which a fine litter of nine newly farrowed pigs perished. First it was the smell that attracted him. He stooped down to feel the pig and burned his fingers; putting them to his mouth he tasted *crackling*! The number of houses on fire for some time afterwards was enormous.

Which leads us on to Suffolk hams that still travel as a great Suffolk accomplishment as far as Harrods in one of their wonderful food halls. But if it is boiled pork you fancy, then surely pease pudding is a great additive. As for me I would go for the pork and onion dumpling, not forgetting the little cap before tying it up.

A beefsteak pudding is a sure standby, but the ingredients are rather more expensive in these days than when our forebears asked for a second helping. But if the first courses were a bit thin we might have recourse to Sir Charles Rowley's plum pudding. However, we would not be able to go back to work on it, so it could only be for Sundays. As for strawberry and raspberry Fool, that served an all too short existence, because if you put it in the fridge you would spoil it.

I must say I rather laughed when I came across General Forbes's Ginger Beer. The date suggests he was in the Crimea or the Mutiny or both, or even Waterloo. How he came to drinking ginger beer is not told.

You will notice I have said nothing about Suffolk cheese, also known as 'Bang'; because that was a byword not to be dwelt upon.

When cottage folk had to use a communal oven for bread-baking (I think Bakers Lane at Westleton suggest such a place), they might take it in turns to have sole use, but for small households, two or three women would combine. To distinguish their respective loaves one woman would pinch a little knob of dough on her loaves, the other two such knobs, the third three, so there would be no dispute. One supposes the children would vie for the crusty knobs. And do you remember when they baked quartern loaves, or sent children to ask for such at the bakers?

For the open air, and the labourer lucky enough to have a bloater, a good way to cook it was to wrap it round in several thicknesses of brown paper, set alight to the paper and when burnt through, the bloater was done to perfection. The paper peeled off quite easily.

And this as a tail-piece from the *Daily Telegraph*, 8th May 1978: "Many aspects of society are likely to be transformed almost beyond recognition by the accelerating advances of the micro-electronics industry.

"Life at home and at work are likely to be transformed within the next few decades. Household computers designed, so that almost any housewife can operate them, will perform such chores as cooking the breakfast, running the bath, laying the table with robotic arms etc." *et al.*

9

The Old Landscape of Brewing

They sell good beer at Haslemere
And under Guildford Hill.
Hilaire Belloc

It is not without interest to consider the influence on the landscape of England which the brewing of beer brought about. Beer was not only the national beverage, but its ingredients were endemic to our native fields; in its processes often purifying the poor drinking water and providing a food and sustenance without which the hard and strenuous manual labour could not have been accomplished. Moreover, it had an ecclesiastical background because many of our old country inns can trace back their ownership to the local church.

First then comes the barley and its cultivation, which takes us in the order of things to Plough Monday, the first Monday after Twelfth Day, when the common plough, bedecked with ribbons was taken into the church to be blessed. This signalized that the Christmas holidays were over and it was time to begin work in the fields. In Cawston Church, Norfolk, is an ancient plough-light gallery, bearing an inscription in old English: "God spede the plough: And send us ale-corn enow: Our purpose for to make: Be mery and glade: Wat good ale yis work made." And it was under this gallery that the plough was placed.

Ploughing then, prepared the fields for the barley, or ale-corn, silken in its new green and flaxen in its ripeness, rippling in the wind like the waters of a summer sea. Also barley had to be treated differently to the other crops in the harvesting, as also in the threshing. It was not made into stooks like the wheat and the oats, but was left to lie in swaithes and had to be gathered into armfuls, usually by the labourer's wife. A clause in the old agreements made at harvest, which were entered into as binding contracts by the taking of 'earnest money', that each man had to provide his own gaveller for this purpose who was usually his wife or a female relation. The proficiency of some of these women is summed up in the epithet bestowed on one such as 'Barley Bess', since her activity in that direction was great. And of course the crop gave rise to the folk-song of "John Barleycorn". When the crop came to the threshing floor it was spread out like a carpet and a barley hummeller was run over it like a garden roller. This served to remove the awms, ails or beards from the grain. Other names of this machine were fothering iron or piling iron. Another form used rammer fashion was known as a thumper, huller or chumper. Sometimes a scuffle was used, which was more like a wooden harrow.

Next came the hop fields of England, mostly concentrated in Kent, but once common to Surrey, with Farnham as a centre, Worcestershire, Herefordshire in the west, and even as far north as Lincolnshire. Also a few in the Stowmarket area of Suffolk.

There used to be an old saying:

> Till St James's day is come and gone,
> There may be hops and there may be none.

And the hop-grower's prayer comes to mind: that he may have a good crop of hops and his neighbour none.

One connects a picture of Kent as much with an oast house as with cherry orchards. Those characteristic circular buildings with conical roof ending in a cowl, looking like the distinguishing features of a French château. One imagines they were always there, at least since hops were first cultivated in this country as far back as the early sixteenth century. But they really only date from the 1830s when a certain John Read introduced them. Yet, peculiarly enough they are more or less native to Kent since those of the west have mostly square houses. Although I expect one can find square houses in Kent and round houses in the west. In those earlier days a good hop-drier who knew his kiln was as essential as a good shepherd or horseman.

The oast-house connotes the hop pocket, once upon a time trodden in by foot, a most exhausting job with few able to stand the strain; the bagging machine did not make an appearance until about the time of the Great Exhibition of 1851. When I was young, the way to the Borough Market and the old Hop Exchange passed through a bottle-neck at Bromley, Kent. The great wains crept through laden with their towering loads.

The pickers, that raggle-taggle band, left their rookeries in London for a Kentish holiday. Their numbers grew year by year until in 1900 it was recorded that 50,000 went from Houndsditch. The old tally sticks they used, notched as they filled each bushel-basket, are now museum pieces.

Then comes the maltster with his wooden spade, cut out from the solid, used instead of iron to prevent breaking the hops made brittle by drying. Those old men were proud of their malting floors: "I can wet seventy-five quarters at once", was the proud boast of one.

The old maltings not only sound nice and biscuity but look pleasant enough where they have survived. The enormous expanse of sagging roof creeping into the scene, providing a catslide of tiles or slates; and the impressive towers brooding against the sky. They had figured amongst the outbuildings of the old manor houses and Halls.

Some years ago now I met an old man well over ninety sitting in the sun of a Suffolk village, who I found quite willing to talk. "No," he said, "I never did smoke. Yes, I drink when I can git a-howd on't." (I put that to the test before I left and noticed the alacrity with which he toddled off to the inn.) "I

5 The travelling trunk of Lady Katherine Grey from Cockfield Hall, Yoxford

6 Darsham Mill

7 Rev. Francis Cunningham, husband of Richenda

8 Richenda Cunningham

was a hossman," he continued, "wi' fower hosses. We'd start at fower or half arter three an' go tew Halesworth maltings. There wur nine men thare wi' red caps, an' praps thare 'ud be tharty wagons." I discovered the early start was to get into the queue as near the front as possible and so be able to return home with another load such as cake or maize, which added a trifle to their wages.

The mention of the maltster's red-stocking cap is interesting and raises the question why certain articles of dress became traditional to the various crafts. For instance the carpenter's paper cap and the butcher's blue apron.

Too many of the old malt houses have passed into oblivion. There was one at Crondall, Hampshire that was thatched and had probably stood there since Tudor times. It supplied quantities from half a gallon for the cottage to a sack for the farmer. A circular house adjoined where a horse walked round and round grinding the malt. Amongst the possessions here was a large pack-saddle used on a horse to take the malt to outlying houses where the roads were too bad for a vehicle.

Malting is essentially a country industry, requiring a skill which almost amounted to an intuition. The complex, incomprehensible chemical processes induced into or out of the grain by men ignorant of the forces they encouraged, but skilful in knowing what was required, seems to enter the realm of inspiration. The hop-drier, the maltster and brewer constituted a trinity of skill, serving a common end.

10

Family Treasures

Some years ago I was presented with an old wooden box that contained certain papers, not of my own family, but of collaterals through my mother's mother. I went through them with considerable enjoyment.

First of all, the box is an exact replica of an eighteenth-century yeoman's chest that would have contained his clothes, with at one end near the top a tray. This would be for his bits of jewellery and more valuable personal belongings. In this case it is to all intents and purposes a deed box of wood, with a hasp lock, and measures 14 ins long, by 6½ ins wide and stands 5½ ins high. The body is of pine, the top is an adzed piece of elm and the mouldings are of mahogany.

The first will, or copy thereof, is a parchment dated 1789, wherein "I Richard Smith of the Hamlet of Wimblington in the parish of Doddington in the Isle of Ely, and county of Cambridge, farmer", leaves his all to his only daughter Elizabeth, near about the age of 11 years, under care of two guardians," to bring her upp and see that she is brought up in a decent manner as a child ought to be brought upp in".

This was proved on the first day of January 1790, before the "Reverend Abraham Jobson, Clerk, our lawful Surrogate".

Imagine my surprise on meeting my namesake of long ago, with whom I can claim no relationship. Was he rubicund of appearance, living well out of the Consistory Court of Ely, or pale and ascetic in appearance from perusing too many of those dry as dust parchments? Alas, we shall never know. As the will was sworn under £40, I am afraid it would not have carried poor little orphan Elizabeth very far in life.

Now comes the copy of a will made by a Sarah Tokelove in 1794, wherein she uses a delightful old word: "And all that my Messuage where I now dwell, together with the Shop and Homestall adjoining, be let to an undeniable tenant or tenants & the rents and profits arising therefrom to be applied to the Cloathing Maintenance & Education of my said son John and my said daughter Amy till she come to the age of Twenty one Years or day of Marriage."

"Homestall" was a synonym for a house and linked humanity in its origins with the 'beasts of the stall' as in the carol.

Articles of Agreement come next, dated 1804, between Thomas and John Tokelove of Doddington, grocers, and Henry and John Lister of Upwell, farmers, of premises for £36 to be paid half yearly – on Lady Day and Michaelmas Day, old style, in every year. The said Henry and John, or either of them, shall use, occupy, manure and cultivate the said land in good and husbandlike manner, according to the custom of the said Field".

A "True copy" of Mr Thomas Tokelove's will follows, dated 5th January 1804, and proved 21st October 1807.

"First I give and devise all my freehold and copy-hold messuages, lands, tenements etc, to my son John Tokelove . . . provided he lives to attain the age of twenty-one years." He had to pay his mother a rent charge of £45 during the term of her life, by two equal payments at the "two usual feasts, Viz, The Feast of the Annunciation of the blessed Virgin Mary and Saint Michael the Archangel". This, in 1804, smacks of pre-Reformation times.

The widow was to have and use the enjoyment of the "best parlour, cellars, kitchen, tub-house, cole house and garden, *with the rooms over the same* where I now live . . ." Also "of all the stock, goods and effects before given to my said son and that with such stock she shall carry on in a fair way of business the trade of a general shopkeeper which I now carry on in Doddington. . . . And I do hereby expressly will and devise that the provision herein before made for the benefit of my said wife in manner aforesaid, is and shall be accepted and taken in lieu full satisfaction of her Dower or Thirds, or, claim in respect thereof."

Sad to relate there is a pencil note in the wide margin to say that son John died 24th July 1817, aged nineteen, and that his sister died about June 1821, leaving no issue.

In 1806 a Mr Manley's Opinion was sought (costing two guineas) about matters arising out of Sarah Tokelove's will of 1794. She did not carry out her husband's instructions about the paying off a mortgage on some land, but bought a further 18 acres instead. Also a dispute arose between her son John when he came of age and his guardian, who had spent more money on his sister Amy. The opinion was that John had a case, but Mr Manley suggested an amicable arrangement instead. However, the next document is a general release of her brother John, from her guardianship made by Miss Amy Tokelove when she was nineteen. She reached her majority and received the sum of £35 10s. 5¼d. By this she "remised, relieved and for ever discharged the said John Tokelove of and from all actions, suits, claims and demands both in Law and in Equity from the beginning of the world to the day of the date thereof".

Now follows the copy of Mrs Ann Faile's will, late of Upwell, dated 31st December 1813. She had one son and seven daughters. One of the latter had married a John Tokelove and another, deceased, had become a Sarah Amerson. She had left three children, a daughter Margaret and two sons, Stephen and John.

Mrs Faile left one eighth of her estate to her son, and the remainder to be divided into seven equal parts, six to her daughters, and the one part to the three grandchildren. On a separate piece of paper there is a list of the seven parts of the silver, including a marrow spoon in one lot.

Mrs Ann Tokelove, widow, made her will on 14th March 1823, and died on 19th October 1828, aged sixty-six years. In it she left everything to her sister Alice Burrows for the term of her natural life. Alice died the next year, on 10th July 1829, aged fifty-seven.

Ann Tokelove evidently had a weak spot for a niece, Sarah, daughter of John Tokelove of Upwell. "I direct that my sister will not dispose of any furniture in the room called The Chintz Room, it being my wish that after her decease it should be delivered up to the said Sarah Tokelove."

We now move to the will of the aforementioned Sarah Tokelove, spinster, made in 1835. In this she "gives and devises unto my dear mother Hannah Tokelove, all my messuage, land, tenements and premises with the yard and orchard opposite in Upwell aforesaid given me by the will of my late father and devised to him by my grandfather".

To close the list comes "An inventory and appraisement of the Household Furniture and other effects of the late Mr John Tokelove of Upwell in the county of Norfolk, deceased, taken the 8th day of January, 1834 by Mr Robert Tiffin, auctioneer and appraiser, and Mr Thomas Hodson.

"In the shop or room as was occupied as a shop, containing a few shop fittings and turf, £2. Kitchen contents £2. Keeping Room with 4 windsor chairs and a wainscot table, together with a Toast Horse £5.10.0. Cellar 10/-, Parlour with a wainscot Card Table and do Dining Table, wines and spirits £30, Best Chamber £15, Back Chamber £10, Servants Room £5.10.0 Plate £6., Horse £10."

But the prize piece of these papers is a little MS 8½ ins by 5 ins consisting of four double sheets of handmade paper, sewn together in a most professional manner, and written with a beautiful clear hand by a quill pen, viz "A Short History of Upwell", 1827. The contents may well have been culled from Blomefield's *Norfolk*. It was in all probability the work of a Sarah Amerson. It commences:

Upwell, lies in the hundred and a half of Clackclose on the western part of Norfolk, together with Outwell, but although the greater part is in Norfolk still a considerable part is in the Isle of Ely. On the dissolution of religious houses, the hundred was separated from the half hundred. . . . The church is a handsome pile of buildings, dedicated to St Peter, consisting of a nave and two aisles. It has a wooden roof with numerous projecting figures of angels, their wings expanded, beautifully carved. . . . In this church is a handsome brass eagle, supported by three lions, which is placed over the Clerk's seat as a desk. . . . In the tower of the church hang six large bells, with a town clock, and on the face are the words "Go about your business and waste not your time". On the old door are several swans carved, probably as a rebus, signifying some benefactor of that name. . . . There was formerly a screen removed about seven years since, and in its place a new gallery erected which divides the chancel from the nave, whereon was painted our Saviour bearing the Cross, the ascension, the descent of the Holy Ghost on the apostles, the Trinity, and an altar with a cup and wafer supported by two bishops. . . . In the chancel is a marble grave stone with a plate of brass, on which is a portrait of the man and his wife, behind the man kneel seven sons, and behind the wife four daughters. These represent the eleven children of Sinalphus Bell, Esq., and Jane his wife.

In the churchyard is an inclosure, surrounded by iron rails, to the memory of the Rev. Hugh James, a former rector. It is stated that he inclosed this piece of ground for himself and family, as thinking it a custom of too much presumption and too little piety, to defile the house of God with the contemptible carcase of sinful men. Mr James married Philippa, of the ancient and honourable family of Hobarts, near Loddon in Norfolk.

Here also is a priory of Gilbertians, dedicated to the Virgin Mary, it was a cell of Sempringham in Norfolk, founded in the reign of King John.

This is a very populous and extensive village called by Dugdale Welle, but was before called Wylla, A.D. 1338, as having its site on a river, viz the ancient Nene, which divides the counties of Norfolk and Cambridge.

There is an ancient building near the church bridge of Upwell which by its appearance seems, and is generally supposed, to have formerly belonged to some chapel or guild. It is the last house in Upwell on the road to Outwell. . . . What strengthens the idea of its having been an ancient religious house is that there is a road or drove way adjoining still called Pious Drove.

The Rev Gale Townley, the rector, has established and endowed a free school for the instruction of boys and girls from eight to eleven years of age, in useful learning.

James Lee, Esq., (A.D. 1819) erected five almshouses for the like number of poor widows, each to have ten bushels of coal at Christmas, besides their living free of rent in the house. The same gentleman has purchased a fire Engine for the use of the parish.

There was formerly a quakers' chapel in this town, situated about a quarter of a mile south-east of the church. The burial ground is still preserved, wherein are some memorials of the interment of persons of that persuasion. A devise of some land lying in Fakenham, in Norfolk was left to poor persons of that belief.

There are two water pumps in this parish given for its convenience & benefit, one stands near the church on the new road, the other in a place near the Fire engine House called new-bridge drove. There are two Methodist Chapels in this place, one near the church on the Isle side, the other near the centre of the town on the Norfolk side.

There is also a chapel called the Ranters' Chapel on the right hand from Upwell on the Norfolk side, near the church.

Now follows a list of charities.

Then to add an artistic flourish to this excellent little record, is a pen drawing of the five Almshouses, done with meticulous care by a J. Tokelove. The youthful artist paid due regard to the "heartrending exactitude" of the brickwork. But I cannot understand why five houses have only four chimney stacks.

This naïve little record is of value to local historians because many little bits were then within memory. For example, M. R. James refers to the church as an equally important building with that of Outwell, but mentions that it had not retained so much of the old fittings, having undergone lavish restoration between 1836 and 1842. He says, "The roofs are fine. A screen which had unusual paintings on it has gone. Among the subjects were the Bearing of the Cross, Ascension, Pentecost, and the Trinity."

Munro Cautley in his *Norfolk Churches* refers to the "abominable gallery", but admits it allows a closer inspection of the beautiful roof. He alludes also to the pre-Reformation brass eagle.

Arthur Mee in his *Norfolk* turns the swans on the south door into sixteen pelicans, and Sinalphus Bell into Linalphus, and gives the eagle a comb.

Incidentally, the two villages of Upwell and Outwell in their five-mile length, are described as the longest village in England.

11

Darsham Mill

With them the Seed of Wisdom did I sow,
And with mine own hand wrought to make it grow;
And this was all the Harvest that I reap'd
"I came like water, and like wind I go."
Rubaiyat of Omar Khayyam

Presumably, the old photograph (*see* plate 6) of the splendid old post mill complete with round house in full working order was taken before the First World War, when the horse was the means of transport, as it had been for centuries, and the fields and farms were as my mother had known them as a girl, and as her father and grandfathers had from time out of mind, ploughing sowing, reaping, in fields that had a name.

It is a happy picture of peace and serenity, the old dusty road littered with horse droppings, the age-old gateway, and the children just out of school, blissfully happy. Girls who were never without those old white pinafores, seeking wild flowers in the ditches; one studious boy, overlooked, by chance, by the straw-hatted parson. But note that little house nearby. It evidently holds an engine to work the mill if the wind fails.

One can well imagine the fine old country wagons, drawn by sorrel horses, bringing their burdens along this way. Or the solitary horseman with his one or two sacks, jogging along, sitting sideways. For this mill represents the ultimate in farming. It suggests the stooks in the fields, the stacks in the stackyards and the harvest moon. And almost all villages possessed one, in some cases two or three. When Cobbett made his journey into Ipswich he counted no less than seventeen mills, all painted white.

Surely these beautiful creations were a tribute to those who tilled the fields. It is not without significance that Constable was the son of a miller and was brought up in that tradition. No wonder he could paint a picture of a hay wain, set in an atmosphere that breathed and lived. He could not help himself. And did not Benjamin Britten reach fame in a mill at Snape?

Darsham was, and is, essentially a farming area. It seems to include my mother's village and Yoxford as well. One could see so far from the top of the mill, green in spring, turning to gold, flecked with red by the poppies that persisted from year to year. In the 1879 directory, one note remains that Bristles Green was enclosed in 1851. Did that cause any hardship I wonder?

Not far from the mill is the age-old church with a Norman doorway and a belfry of four bells, one to St Thomas dated 1656, the other three by John Brend. I wonder if they still make music in the quiet air?

The Bedingfields bought the fine old baronial hall known as Darsham Hall, otherwise the Manor House. Now, hardly a vestige remains, but a farmhouse bears its name. They presented to the church in 1616. There is a brass to the memory of Mistress Anne Bedingfield, who died in 1641, aged eighty years and seven months. And there is a monument on the north wall to Sir Thomas Bedingfield, a lawyer, who relinquished all his Crown and public appointments as a protest against the murder of Charles I. He retired to Darsham where he died in 1660. So were our Suffolk villages wrapped up with the history of England.

To confirm the village's association with the fields, Darsham had a hurdle maker. I remember him quite well with his wigwam of poles, his sharp little axe, and his capacity to turn them out all gleaming new, like shelled peas.

But Darsham had something else, to me a magic key, in the shape of a railway station. I can hear those porters yet, calling it out – "Darsham, Daa-rsham!" as we dropped on to the platform full of joy and contentment; and yet again sadly and too soon when the man from the signal box opened the gates to let the London train go through. I felt sad again recently when I went through in a pay-train to see them breaking down the outbuildings of the station that were once so busy, and to notice how everywhere was so overgrown and neglected. But the buildings, low and countrified are still there, that in the old days belonged to George T. Arnott, maltster, corn, coke, salt and manure merchant.

Yes, the signal box has gone, so the tinkling bell has ceased to ring, and there are no lights from his high windows when the dark days are with us. But it was with us when the flying bombs came in from the sea off the Heinkles, because the signalman wondered what they were.

And it was from Darsham Station in the 'seventies of the last century that my mother set out alone, to make one of the million and a quarter of servant girls then so employed. I don't suppose there was anyone to meet her at Shoreditch Station, with her great black box made by the wheelwright and coffin maker for the occasion. She probably didn't know she was destined for a lovely secluded spot in Upper Norwood, that was as beautiful and lovely as this scene at Darsham Mill.

Once upon a time I knew the names of all the stations between our house in south-east London and that Darsham. It was a golden chain, of which some links have been broken by the hand of time. And when, in the dying embers of a visit in those halcyon days of youth, the pony trap was harnessed and waiting, and it was time to leave those scented fields, we could wave a goodbye as we turned right at the rectory corner in Middleton, made our way across the Rackford Run, and get a last glimpse of that old farmhouse, before we clip-clopped into Fen Street, the shortest way to the old station. Perhaps grandfather had a little catch in his throat if he thought of the first time he had seen off that daughter of his, my mother, on her way into a new unchartered world.

Ah, the good days of coaching are past like a dream
And we, the crack dragsmen, are victims of steam;
There are many good fellows have cause to bewail
The old line of road and the new line of rail.

12

Lowestoft St Margaret's

The High Street is one mile in length.

The question has been raised as to why the Church of St Margaret is so far from the centre of the town. It may well be because it stands on such a commanding site, one of the highest points in the district.

Munro Cautley tells us that it is chiefly fifteenth century, though the tower with its spire is probably a century earlier. The windows and buttresses are not only very fine but very unusual. The appearance inside is also very fine with its slender pier arcade and roof carried through without a break from end to end.

And this is what M. R. James remarks: "This old church, remote from the town, is large and dignified: it contains a good brass eagle, a font with pairs of figures on the bowl, much broken, and the matrix of a brass of a good old man, Thomas Scrope, a Carmelite, bishop of Dromore in Ireland (d. 1491) – he wrote books about his Order, led a very ascetic life, and died at the age of 100."

Of course, St Margaret's Church, in the old town on the cliff has got a history all its own. It is indeed a noble structure and retains old memories. For instance, that little parvise over the south porch, housed two maiden sisters named Elizabeth and Katherine, and is still known as the Maids' Chamber. Their life was devoted to good works, including the sinking of two wells which became known as the Basket Wells, this being a corruption of the mingling of the two names Bess and Kate. They were to be of immediate and lasting value to the local inhabitants when pure water was none too easy to obtain.

Kelly's 1879 directory tells of a thorough restoration of the church in 1871 and of the insertion of a stained-glass window to the memory of a Lady Smith who died in 1877 having completed her 104th year. Born Pleasance Reeve, she had been a great beauty in her time, and on her hundredth birthday she received a copy of *Our Life in the Highlands* from Queen Victoria with Her Majesty's autograph. It also tells of the memorials of that sea then called the German Ocean, and the bunch of Lowestoft Admirals, all of whom have memorials in the church, Allin, Arnold, Ashby, Leake, Mighells and Utber. Not bad for one small place on our Suffolk coast. I don't think anywhere else can equal it.

Naturally smuggling creeps into the story; late one night a sailor called on the vicar, the Rev Francis Cunningham, and begged him to come and see a man on board a ship who was dying. The vicar answered the call and was rowed out to the vessel concerned. He was then asked if he would conduct the burial service early the next morning. To this he agreed also and duly conducted the service in all due solemnity as they wished their mate to be buried in St Margaret's churchyard. Soon after it was discovered that he had read the service over a coffin filled with contraband lace and other goods, and that the men and the corpse had vanished.

I also notice that this very kindly and godly man successfully sued a fisherman for Christ's Dole, a tithe payable to the rector of St Margaret's on fish. The sum amounting to 10s. 3d. for the tithe and 10s. costs. I reckon poor old John Roberts was 'whooly' riled!

Mrs Cunningham was no less a person than Richenda Gurney of Earlham, one of the famous seven sisters who wore red coats, loved dancing and hated Quakerism, and halted the mail by joining hands across the road. Her elder sister was the noted Mrs Elizabeth Fry, the prison reformer and anti-slavery advocate, who *was* a Quaker. However Richenda left off being a

Quaker and joined the Church of England.

One of the clerical friends who became a frequent visitor to Earlham was Francis Cunningham, rector of Pakefield, and in 1815 became engaged to Richenda. They were married at Earlham Church, the bride being given away by her cousin, Hudson Gurney. Like all her married sisters she never ceased to have a close and loving share in the family life at Earlham, but in her happy home at Pakefield and afterwards at Lowestoft, she was the most spirited and devoted clergyman's wife.

Percy Lubbock in his beautiful symphony of a book, *Earlham* imagines what the evening service at Lowestoft must have been like, when the lamps were burning bright, the parishioners came trooping into their seats and the wind moaned without. "All the well known faces. They rise from their knees settle themselves in their places with beaming looks, disposing their wraps and Bibles and hymn-books about them and settle down for an hour's bliss that lasted all week." Lubbock hoped they sang 'Helmsley', with plenty of trailing sweeps to the high notes.

These two were to become the Uncle and Aunt Cunningham of Earlham, she the best beloved of the aunts. Lubbock adds: "The cheerful rectory by the sea was well-known to our grandmother's children, and she herself would be made thrice welcome there."

Richenda had been trained as an artist by no less a person than old Crome, and when in her days before marriage the family went into the Lake District for a holiday, Crome went with them. In describing the gardens at Earlham, Richenda comes back again: "A century ago, then, I should certainly come across Aunt Richenda at this spot (the Sulky Walk), plying her pencil at a great pace. Almost while you wait the page of the sketch-book is covered, and the human interest is not forgotten . . . in the vista she has placed a young woman in a poke bonnet, with a droll little skipping child by her side. For all her sisters and brothers when they go out into the world, carry a little album labelled 'Earlham' filled end to end expressing Richenda's love for her old home." A home, incidentally, that the Gurneys never owned but rented from the Bacon family.

Augustus Hare in his *Gurneys of Earlham* tells of a visit to Lowestoft: "We spent a delightful time in that unusual home; no other place is like it in its freedom, its wonderful activity, its thoughtful kindness, in the truly parental care over everybody. Everything is marked by generosity and truest charity. It was amusing as we walked through the town, to see the greetings with the children, the smiles and loving words, varied by a hard shaking and sharp lecture to a vulgar girl swinging on a chain and showing her legs." (!)

> There was a charm in Mrs Cunningham's character which gave her a strong hold upon all with whom she came in contact . . . Lowestoft Vicarage was an open house. Her face and voice are inseparably connected with the Sunday hymn-singing at the Vicarage, a famous institution in those days. Between the five o'clock tea and the seven o'clock evening service, it was customary to assemble the household, the pupil-teachers and others who formed the choir, and any others who liked to attend, in the drawing room to sing hymns and anthems. Mrs Cunningham presided at the piano and led the party with her high clear voice, her face beaming with faith and joy.

One day when the vicar was reading family prayers, a servant burst in with, "Please sir, your study's on fire." "All right James," was the reply, "but this is not the time to speak of such things"; and went on reading the chapter and the prayers. The study was burnt out.

Returning to Richenda, writing to her sister Lady Buxton, who was not always in affluent circumstances: "I have been laughing at the remembrance of those days when you lived in a cottage, and I used to save up all the sixpences and shillings I could scrape together for you."

And in Lady Buxton's words: "To my sister Richenda any place seems a garden, no spot is barren to her; there is no wilderness in her life; her mind's eye sees flowers everywhere."

Richenda died peacefully, 15th August 1855, having been visited for the last time only two days before her death by her brother Samuel, "her prince of brothers", as she always called him. She is buried at Lowestoft. Mr Cunningham died in August 1863: "it was a departure in complete beatitude".

Earlham was a great home to all the family even when they were dispersed. Elizabeth Fry recalls the exclamation of an old friend who saw a happy united circle gathered at Earlham and exclaimed: "What! all this and heaven besides!"

One other interesting thing happened to Mrs Fry on one of her frequent visits to the old home. She was summoned to the death bed of a Norfolk squire, who was nearly related to her; he remarked: "I am very glad to see thee, Elizabeth and shall be very glad to talk with thee; but thee must just wait till these have done!" On the other side of the bed were two cocks fighting.

North Norfolk was rather populated by the Gurneys. They had a house at Cromer and were settled in at Northrepps Hall. They were known as the 'cottage ladies-- Miss Anna Gurney and Miss Sarah Buxton. They held Sunday evening meetings in the old Hall to which the Overstrand fishermen sometimes came. It was due to the energies of Miss Anna that Hasbro' lighthouse was established, because of the great number of shipwrecks on that often stormy coast.

A contemporary letter tells of Sarah Buxton's funeral at the ivy-clad ruins of Overstrand Church:

> I cannot describe the luxuriance of beauty at the Cottage. The greenness was dazzling in the brilliant sun, the lawn gay with dahlias and scarlet geraniums, the fern-hill gay and beautiful, nature in perfection. But how things are mingled! Between the pond and Cottage stood a multitude composed of her school-children, boys and girls; the former in black pinafores, the latter in black frocks (poor mites), and their teachers and fishermen without number.

At last the hearse appeared, crossing the lawn from the garden-door. We all fell in behind, with the children forming a line up each side, singing as we crossed that beautiful sloping field and ascended the lane. The Cromer people joined us on the way, her Bible Committee, and almost everyone else. It was unlike any other funeral: there was something joyous in it, the hymns and the country seemed to bring heaven so near. Then we all went into the church, the coffin first, borne by twelve fishermen, full of grief. Next came cousin Anna in her chair. The tiny church was crowded, every one in black, and beautiful were the old ruins, with the grand sea through the broken arches, a place of perfect quiet and rest. The vault was open, and dearest Harry's coffin before our eyes. Cousin Anna sat at the end of the vault, between it and the church, Spinks and Stephen leaning on the back of her chair, looking as if their hearts would break, and all the maids behind them. The ruins were crowded besides the churchyard. When the service was ended, there was a moment's pause, and then Uncle Cunningham stood on a gravestone, without his gown, and with the sun shining through the ruins on his head, and spoke to us, describing her character, her spirituality, her hopefulness, her charity, and her close faithfulness to all around her.

And this is what they wrote of her in a charming little booklet published in 1936 in aid of the Cromer and District Hospital: "In the spring the foothills are covered with that wonderful haze of purply blue from the wild hyacinth before the brakefern hides it, and in May the rhododendrons flame round the old home of Anna Gurney, one of the finest characters of an earlier time."

13

A Journey through Suffolk with Thomas Dugdale, Antiquarian

Will the day's journey take the whole long day?
From morn to night, my friend.

Christina Rossetti

I have amongst my books the seven volumes on England and Wales published in the very early years of the nineteenth century by this delightful old antiquarian, assisted by William Burnett. Recently I searched through them to see what he had to say about our county and was intrigued by his naïvety. He seems to have noted all the fairs, so I was very pleased to look over his shoulder. As for some of the small towns they would hardly recognize themselves; but the period covers the years of my Suffolk grandfather, although he would not have had a wider range of acquaintance than about ten miles from his village of Middleton. Time has passed all too quickly for anyone to recall those early days, even when generations lie behind many memories deep.

All the villages are noted, with distances from here to there, but only those that stand out by reason of something peculiar about them call for notice. In some cases he only notices the fairs, and I was particularly struck with the number of these which sold toys. I have been always led to believe our grandparents as children had a thin time, but it would appear otherwise from this toy trade. I wonder who made them – who bought them – who cherished them? Were they of foreign origin or just from Suffolk? Alas we shall never know.

Incidentally, and as a digression, the day I am writing this a nineteenth-century toy train-set, without its engine, fetched £2,900 at Christie's, South Kensington, yesterday. True it dates from 1895, outside the scope of these country fairs, but the extraordinary fact remains of interest in these youthful delights.

Of course there are other things mentioned by Dugdale besides toys, and their nomenclature gives us a delightful glimpse into past requirements. I wonder if folks favoured with such knowledge knew where to get just this or that? One thing more, take note of the dates, the Christian year looms large, not forgetting that Whitsuntide of which we have been deprived, with all its joyful country attributes appears; and the old calendar gave that great day of settlement-Michaelmas as 11th October and not September as now.

Let us then go on our tour, remembering the roads are often muddy, rutted and rough under foot. But the air is sweet and the roadside verges are alive with wild flowers that have not lost their fragrance. Of these, of course, the scarlet poppy will be much in evidence. Moreover, our jaunts will be strictly governed by the alphabet, so we begin with A.

Ashfield Great. This obscure village gave birth to the celebrated Lord Chancellor Thurlow and his brother, the late Bishop of Durham; they were the sons of the vicar. The former was never married, but he left three illegitimate daughters, to two of whom he bequeathed large property; the other having offended him by an imprudent marriage, he left only a small annuity.

Beccles. Near this town is a large common, on which the inhabitants of the town have the privilege of feeding their cattle on easy terms. [Not, of course, what you and I understand by the term.]

Fairs. Whit Monday, June 29 and October 2 for horses and pedlery.

Bildeston Fairs, Ash Wednesday and Holy Thursday [when it rained curative holy water], wearing apparel and toys.

Bungay. In the market place which is considered the best in the county, are two crosses under one of which fowls and butter are exposed for sale, and under the other corn and grain. The castle, once the residence and stronghold of the Bigods, Earls of Norfolk . . . has become the habitation of helpless poverty; many miserable hovels having been reared against its walls for the accommodation of the lowest classes. . . . The principal streets leading to Norwich, Yarmouth, Bury and Ipswich are broad and well paved. . . . Here is also a free grammar school, which enjoys the right of sending two scholars to Emmanuel College, Cambridge. The springs of this place are supposed to possess medicinal qualities of great efficacy.

Fairs. May 14 for horses and lean cattle; and September 25 for hogs and petty chapmen. [I like the last touch.]

Bury St Edmunds is the next stop, otherwise known as the Montpelier of England. We are warned that the air, though extremely fine for persons of robust constitution, is too sharp for those who *enjoy* a delicate state of health. (Even some of the old Suffolk labourers did that for they were never above being 'middling'). "The Angel Inn, one of the most conspicuous buildings in the town, stands on the west side of Angel Hill. The vaults underneath it are supposed to have formerly belonged to the abbey, and to have once had a subterraneous communication with that establishment." And why not since the monks brewed their own beer? Suffolk was full of subterraneous passages when I was young, and I did not think much of any ruin that had not got one. But what would the Angel have been without Sam Weller and Mr Pickwick?

Not far from the east gate of the abbey stood St Nicholas' hospital, some remains of which are yet to be seen converted into a farm house. Just without the South-gate was the hospital of St Petronella; the chapel of which, still pretty entire, is now used as a malt house. [Alas Time carries all away.]

Fairs, Easter Tuesday, October 2, for three weeks, for butter, cheese and millinery [note the mixture], December 1 for cattle.

Clare, Fairs Easter Tuesday and July 29 for toys.

Debenham. The town is meanly built, but the church is

handsome. Sir Robert Hitcham directed in his will that twenty poor children should be instructed in his school at Framlingham; but that being found inconvenient a master was appointed at Debenham.

Fairs, June 24 for braziery and toys. [My dictionary gives a brazier as one who works in brass. So could it have been the old copper kettles or the old brass candlesticks so highly prized by our ancestors?]

Dunwich. Sprats are cured here in the same manner as herrings are at Yarmouth. Fairs, July 25 for toys.

Brent Eley, now a village, was once a market town, and long the seat of the Colman family, one of whom built and furnished with books, a parochial library, and another endowed a neat almshouse for six persons.

Eye. The principal manufacture is in bone lace. Fairs, Whit Monday for cattle and toys.

Flixton. The church here is in ruins, its roof having been blown off in the great storm, November 27, 1703. The walls have been applied to the building of stables, and the font having been split asunder supports the two ends of a hog-trough.

Fornham All Saints. Out of lands in this neighbourhood, Penelope, Countess of Rivers gave a rent charge of £8 per annum that a sermon might be preached four times a year against popery.

Framlingham. Fairs, Whit-Monday and October 11th for cattle, sheep and cloth.

Fressingfield. The deposed Archbishop of Canterbury, Dr William Sancroft was born and died here. In his will he left £52 p.a. to the vicar and his successors for ever on condition he should pay £10 p.a. to the master of the school he had founded there, and £6 p.a. to the parish clerk, for whom and his successors for ever.

Hacheston. Fairs, November 12 for boots, upholstery and joiners work.

Haverhill. Fairs, May 12 and October 26 for toys.

Honington. An obscure village, is celebrated as the birthplace of the pastoral poet Robert Bloomfield. His mother kept a school in a cottage near the church, where she died in 1804. At the age of thirteen or fourteen he was received by his brothers to be instructed in their trade of shoemaking. At that time his knowledge of books was so small that he was at a loss to comprehend the meaning of words that commonly occur in the newspaper; but by a process of study unexampled in the annals of literature, and astonishing to those who witness its traces in his writings, his diction, like his understanding and poetical genius, became strong, flowery and perspicuous. His principal production is the Farmer's Boy, a poem displaying most of the beauties belonging to that species of composition, strength, sweetness, harmony of numbers and simplicity. He also published a volume of Rural Tales, Ballads and Songs, and several other productions, which are all possessed of a merit peculiar to his writings.

Ipswich. The streets in general are narrow, and disposed without much attention to regularity. The Orwell which is noted for its beauty, affords the means for pleasant excursions to Harwich, and to that place wherries go and return regularly every tide.

Fairs, May 4 and 19 for lean cattle and toys, July 25 for toys; August 22 for horses and lambs; September 25 for butter and cheese.

Ixworth. Fairs, Whit-Monday for toys.

Landguard or Langer Fort. Fresh water is conveyed thither by pipes from Walton, a distance of about three miles.

Lavenham. Fairs, Shrove Tuesday and October 10 for butter and cheese.

Leiston. This place is remarkable for the ruins of an abbey of Premonstratensian canons, which was founded in 1182; great part of the church, several subterranean chapels and other offices are still standing, and are used as barns and granaries.

Lowestoft. Situated on a lofty headland bordering on the German Ocean, and said to be the most easterly point of land in South Britain, the difference in time here from the Observatory at Greenwich being seven minutes. Fairs, May 12 St Michael and October 10 for petty chapmen.

Long Melford. On Cranmer Green in this parish is a petrifying spring. Fairs, Whit-Tuesday for pedlery. Wednesday and Thursday for cattle and sheep.

Mendlesham. Towards the end of the seventeenth century, an ancient silver crown was dug up here, which weighed about sixty ounces, and supposed to have belonged to one of the kings of the East Angles. Fair, October 2 for cattle.

Mildenhall. Henry Barton, Lord Mayor of London in 1428 and

William Gregory in 1451 were both natives of this town. [Worth a mention.] Fair, October 10 for wool.

Nayland. A small market town situated on the north bank of the Stour over which it has a large brick bridge of one arch leading into Essex. The river is navigable from Sudbury to Harwich, by which means corn and flour are carried to Mastley [*sic*] for the port of London, whence coal is brought back again. Fair, October 2 for horses, cattle and toys.

Needham Market. Fairs, October 28 for toys.

Newmarket. On the 22 March 1683, during the races, the town was nearly destroyed by an accidental fire, which occasioned the hasty departure of the Company then assembled including the king, the queen, the Duke of York, and their attendants; and to this disaster historians have ascribed the failure of the Rye-House Plot, the object of which is stated to have been the assassination of the king and his brother on the road from Newmarket to London, if the period of the journey had not been anticipated. Fairs, Whit-Tuesday and November 8 for horses and sheep.

Orford. On the south-east of this parish is a lighthouse, which together with another in the parish of Sudbourne are called the Orfordness lights. Fairs, Midsummers day, June 24 for toys.

Rendlesham. Rendlesham House is a princely residence, surpassed by few in the kingdom. It gives its title of an Irish baron to the family of Thelluson.

Saxmundham. A market town supposed to be of Saxon origin, situated in a valley near a small stream which flows into the Alde. The town has no particular manufactures, and the chief article of its trade is salt. Considerable quantities of iron are also shipped to London. The houses are in general well built, but the streets are narrow and unpaved. Fairs, Whit-Tuesday and first Thursday in October for toys.

Monk Soham. The chief produce of this place is from the dairies, and cheese, in quality like to that of Stilton is made here. Fair, May 7 for cows and horses.

Earl Soham. Fair, August 4 for lambs.

Southwold. Large quantities of red herrings and red sprats are cured here and salt manufactured and exported hence. Malt is also an article of considerable importance in the transactions of the place. This part of the coast is remarkable for the arrival and departure of swallows. Fairs, Trinity Monday and August 24 for toys.

Stoke [by Nayland]. Here was formerly a monastery to which Earl Alfgar and his daughters Aethelfled and Aegelfled made considerable donations, it being the burial place of the family. Fairs, February 25; Whit-Monday; May 12 for toys.

Stow Market. Many of the inhabitants are employed in the manufacture of sacking, ropes, twine etc which has succeeded that of stuffs and bombazines. The House of Industry has every appearance of a gentleman's seat. [I wonder if the inmates thought so.] Fairs, July 10 for shop goods and toys. August 12 for sheep and cattle, and a cheese fair in September.

Sudbury. Fairs, March 12, July 10, September 4; for earthenware, glass and toys.

Woodbridge. Fairs, April 5 and October 31 for cattle.

14

Period Pieces

On the contrary, I think a young man might be very safely recommended to take Mr Elton as a model. Mr Elton is good-humoured, cheerful, obliging, and gentle. He seems to me to be grown particularly gentle of late.

Jane Austen, Emma.

We hardly realized when he lived among us and resided in the seclusion of the Hall that he was the last lord of the manor that we should know. Like so many other things, we took him for granted, and in that we were hardly to blame because he had been of us all his life, for his father – the lord before him – had died when he was nine. Therefore ever since the years of pupilage he had succeeded and occupied the ancient and honourable office of lord of our manor. But now, like the miller, the parish clerk, the parish constable, the travelling tailor and the clock-maker, he has gone and we are that much the poorer.

He loved our village as he loved his own park. Not the slightest bit of alteration or decay was allowed if he had the power to prevent it; and we have been living on his care and solicitation ever since. If the village contains much that we would desire, then it is he we have to thank. So much in his affection did he hold the village and his home, that he wrote a book on the subject which is a model for would-be local historians. Not a tree in his park but was a bosom friend; so much so that he was wont to go to a little excess in his estimations of these lively splendours. As for instance when Baker Free was performing his annual cut of the hay, he was seen to break off a small branch as he passed under it with his machine. Out comes our lord with a remonstrance. "Well, master," argued Baker, "thet wur in my way an' wud ha' give me a clout o' the hid."

"Never mind your head, Free", came the swift reply. "Don't you damage my trees." A bit hard perhaps, but it showed where his affections lay.

From which you might infer that he had no care for the labouring classes and the poor, but in that you would err. His fine spare form could be seen about our ways on some errand or other, on foot or on horseback, wearing his inseparable monocle. (In fact his monocle was a kind of weather or temper vane, as far as he was concerned. If all was well it rested in his eye, placidly and shiningly, but if upset it popped in and out twenty times a minute.) If there was a case of illness or distress he would know. And he did not stop to ask if they could do with 'suffen'. If money, or coals, or woollen blankets, or a few clothes, a bottle of wine or brandy would ease the pain and the difficulty, well it came promptly and with such kindness. If he could not come himself, then he sent the parson. And some of his best friends were numbered amongst those poor honest humble folk that made up a community in those days.

One in particular, William Pipe, our last parish clerk shared his secrets and his thoughts. For if the squire seemed to know all about William, it is certain that William knew all about the squire.

Of course, our squire had a few peculiarities; he was not all soft-soap and lather. He liked to be acknowledged as the head of the parish; and if the gals forgot to curtsey – which they didn't – or the lads to doff their hats – which they sometimes did – he would take them to task. He and his house came to the service every Sunday morning that he was at the Hall, and would enter the churchyard by the lower little wicket gate. Sometimes, just to test things out, he would walk round to the entrance at the corner and make his way to the south door that way. And if the boys or lads forgot, he would walk up to them with a "Now you fellas, don't you know your manners?"

Always it was he who read the Lessons, his monocle in attendance, as he made his way to the reading desk from the family aisle with its ornate bench-ends, escutcheons and windows that he had built at great expense, not without involving some criticism.

He did his best for the boys of the village. They came to the Hall to learn fret-work, basket making, or some other useful craft, once a week, under the supervision of his daughters. But woe betide them if he saw them picking his daffodils on the way in or out. If they had asked him all would have been well, but to take liberties was another matter. If so be when they grew up they had a mind to go into the army or navy, then he would see to that. Off they would go to Shotley or Aldershot, and there was no return other than in uniform. He had a weak spot for the Services – having been a sailor himself – and could read ominous signs not apparent to others of his time. His sons were to follow into both spheres and do him credit – one to become an admiral, the other to gain a posthumous V.C. at Gallipoli. No bad contribution to the well being of one's home and country.

The grounds of the Hall were open to all and sundry at certain times of the year. The lawn, as it was called, that stretched towards the west side of the house, was covered with cowslips, and in the spring of the year, when these hung their yellow 'blows' in freshness, folks would go and gather as many as they would; but must spare the jonquils. In fact a public footpath ran across the park and came out by the Round House that was haunted. As there was a great taste for wine of home-made vintage in those days, the privilege was fully indulged and many a bottle glistened in a winter's firelight as a result of that spring and that lawn. Then at the flowering of the year, when all the crops were gathered, and the stubbles showed where heavy sheaves had stood, the farmers and their men, their women and their children came here for the great occasion of the rural cycle – the annual harvest home. And what a to-do that was to be sure. It took a week to get ready, and Pipe was chief man in those preparations. Once they went so far as to let off some fireworks from the roof of the Hall, and the old gals felt sure the end of the world "worn't far away; p'raps thet 'ud be afoor tew morrer"!

They boiled the great plum puddings in Pipe's copper which Mahala, his wife, and Jessie, his daughter, and all the women had been so busy making. ("Be sure yew stoon them raisins, gal, or mind yew git them eyes out o' them taters.") They boiled and roasted the meat, for there were both. A bit of salt beef, or roast pork, or leg of mutton or a shin of beef. ("Dew yew think we ha' gort enow, partner?") And then when the day came and the marquees were erected the little old pony cart would be running backwards and forwards from Pipe's to plate, as fast as it could go. A pint of ale and some tobacco for the men, a pint of stout for the women, and an ounce of snuff for the old gals, of which they were very fond. What a day and what an occasion, with little or nothing left over, and plenty of sniffs and gurgling satisfaction.

Some of course got more than a pint and a bit frisky, and some ate more than was good for them, and were not much use in the games and frolic. But there was a toy for the children who had their meal after the elders. And all kinds of sports for the grown-ups, until you began to realize how good it was to be a countryman under a good squire at the end of a good harvest. And then, yes, at the end, they would have their 'photo's-took' – all the motley throng, grouped about the squire and his family who were plumb in the middle. What an old-fashioned picture they look, to be sure; and yet not so long ago in the history of our times.

Yes, that was a nice old Hall, and yet it was not so old, for one of the earlier squires had taken down the genuine article and had this Palladian effort put up instead, as he liked to be modern. No bathroom, and plenty of work for the maids, but then there were plenty of maids. When the latter were dressed up in their Sunday best, they sometimes had their photos taken, and now you might mistake them for the ladies of the house, although between them was a great gulf fixed. All the water had to be pumped up in the stone-flagged addition to the kitchen, but this was done by the backhouse boy; and then it had to be carted all over the house by hand and the slops brought down.

Cooking was a great art, but there was something to cook, not forgetting venison; and there was all the cleaning to be done. The rooms were furnished with nice bits of eighteenth-century furniture that had not been cast out; but a few bits of heavy monstrous pieces denoted that it was made after the Great Exhibition of 1851 and in the reign of Victoria. The Prince Consort's contribution to the scene was found in the tied cottages. They lived as happily as they could, all in together. Sanitation was poor, but they had a Palladian ballroom, filled with pictures. And you may be sure that a few tales ran around of happenings and events in the cycle of work in running the Hall.

One of these concerned the emptying of the cesspits every four years. What a job that was, once again as so much else in the life of a countryman, governed by the moon. When the moon was full, four men with handcups on long poles, with a hoss and cart, would make their way to the Hall, arriving there at ten o'clock. All the windows would be sealed up, the ladies sent off to bed, and then the pit opened. The squire would come out and give the final review, tell the willing workers they could smoke, give them a bottle of gin, retire himself, and they would set to work until the stable clock struck a tinkling two. Four hours once every four years, for 4s. 6d. apiece. And that was plenty often enough.

Yes, he was a gentleman in every sense of the word, as his wife was a lady. A gentle pair who found a complement in each other. How he laughed at some of the queer characters he knew so well and so intimately, not by hearsay but by personal acquaintance. Such as poor old Aunt Ling, who lived low lying at Tea Pot Hall down by East Bridge. Old Dan Geater lived down there too and they said he could swear longer than any other man thereabouts. My heart! if he got upset, he spilt it as though it were a barrel of beer that had been broached.

And so the squire – the last Lord of the Manor – though he never held a manor court, passed over, as did those whom he called friend and relation and with whom he was wont to commune. They went as they had come, one or two at a time; though not always in the order of their arrival. His wife went first and that was such a grievous loss as he could hardly bear. Down the scale, Mahala also was the first to go, but William followed soon after, though at ninety, and to the last, he showed few signs of failing.

Then went the squire also, almost suddenly, with some of his old friends to mourn his passing. They brought his coffin on a farmcart, drawn by his fine Suffolk Punches, past his trees and along the avenue. At his wish, the boys and girls, each wearing a black bow or 'snoo' lined the pathway to the south door of the church. As they lowered his body into the laurel-lined grave they sang –

May the grace of Christ our Saviour,
And the Father's boundless love,
With the Holy Spirit's favour,
Rest upon us from above.

Thus may we abide in union
With each other and the Lord,
And possess in sweet communion,
Joys which earth cannot afford.

We then knew we had lost the head of our village, as we were all too soon to lose his successor; and the Hall was to fall into vacancy. But they had lived up to their motto on the old hatchments – *Palma non sine pulvera.*

Of a recently published life of Gertrude Bell by H. V. Winstone – who was such a powerful influence in the Middle East during and after the First World War and helped to bring about the Hashemite Kingdom of Iraq – a review in the *Daily Telegraph* has this paragraph:

"The man with whom Gertrude Bell fell in love – reciprocated, but not, on the evidence of surviving letters, consummated – was a regular soldier, Col. Dick Doughty-Wylie, nephew of the explorer Charles Doughty. He was killed at Gallipoli, leading an assault that won him a V.C."

9 Punch and Judy, violinist and steam tram from my museum

10 Elephant, walking doll, singing bird, doll's house and other toys, also from my museum

15

Churchyard Verse

I have just been reading a book on *English Churchyard Memorials* by Frederick Burgess. This, of course, distinguishes between those in the open air, rather than those inside the churches. It also brings to mind the fact that Felixstowe is still a rural area, however much others would make it urban, for we have in our midst a churchyard still in use. A little while ago there were two, but Felixstowe parish church is the sole survivor. However, even in this case most of the interesting inscriptions have become obliterated by the hand of time.

Once upon a time churchyards were the happy hunting grounds of the collector of epitaphs, but this seems to have died out. Howbeit, they still hold a fascination for the rambler into the past, although new discoveries are hardly to be made. In a few years deterioration and the iconoclast will have done their deadly work. The hand of the latter can be seen as near to us at Walton, where a number of most interesting stones have been placed, face upwards on the ground to form paths.

At Letheringham the church and monuments were sold to a builder, some of the fragments being rescued by the Vicar of Brandeston and made into a pyramid in his garden, bearing the inscription, 'Indignant Reader! these monumental remains are not, as thou mayest suppose, the ruins of Time. But were destroyed by an Irruption of the Goths so late in the Christian era as 1789. Credite Posteri.' This was destroyed a few years ago.

Besides eccentricities of verse, these old stone memorials take on a local flavour and a name. It can usually be noted that many came out of the same workshop. Designs may vary, but similarity of treatment suggests a common origin; and in so many cases, splendid workmanship. Before the flood of white marble crosses, angels and other strained efforts, the old churchyards must have been ideal gardens of rest, with mellowing stone, the wooden rails, and the brambled graves of the poor.

> With wicker rods we fenc'd her Tomb around,
> To ward from Man and Beast the hallow'd ground:
> Lest her new Grave the Parson's Cattle razes,
> For both his Horse and Cow the church Yard grazes.

But there was no overcrowding on the north side of the church, which had a certain ominous flavour about it.

> And that I might longer undisturb'd abide,
> I choos'd to be laid on the northern side.

J. C. Loudon, architect, designer of cemeteries, and much else said this: "To the resident poor, uncultivated by reading, the churchyard is their book of history, their biography, their instructor in architecture and sculpture, their model of taste, and an important source of moral improvement."

It must also be noted that modern interest in local history, has found a fruitful field in these churchyard memorials, and much work has been done in recording the inscriptions. When travel was limited, you have the record of a village, even a town, in these peaceful acres. Infantile mortality can be traced, and epidemics, in the line-up of gravestones, even if their tears are shed in stone, and heroic attempts (on others) of new methods of treatment. "At Worth Maltravers, Dorset is buried Benjamin Jesty of Downshay, died 1816, aged 79, born at Yetminster and 'particularly noted for having been the first Person [known] that introduced the Cow Pox by Inoculation, and who from his great strength of mind made the Experiment from the (Cow) on his wife and two sons in the year 1774.'"

One or two facts are brought out in the volume under consideration, viz. the first stone monuments with dedicatory inscriptions and funerary symbolism were introduced into Britain during the time of the Roman occupation. But nothing of this sort has been discovered in Felixstowe, although a number of cinerary jars have been located.

Up to the end of the eighteenth century, the poor were usually buried only in a shroud, tied head and foot. They were carried to the grave on a parish bier and interred without a coffin.

At Dunwich, some thirty miles up the coast from Felixstowe, as the dead emerge from the churchyards on the crumbling cliffs, very large numbers of shroud-pins were picked up on the beach, together with other medieval trifles. This was after what was known as a scouring tide.

Mrs Esdaile, who wrote an important book on church monuments, was of the opinion that the footstone anticipated the headstone, and instanced the ballad in *Hamlet* "at his head a grass-green turf, At his heels a stone", which brings us to Weever's definition of a monument: "Sepulchres should be made according to the qualities and degrees of the person deceased, that by the tombe everyone might be discernd of what ranke he was living." Happily, we are not dealing with rank in our churchyards, save that of growth, but with the ordinary common man who made our towns and villages.

We must remember, however, that in many cases, these inscriptions according to an old writer, in "their fulsomeness and utter want of truth, while praising the departed, outdo anything of that kind in the pagan world itself, so that 'to lie like an epitaph' has grown into a saying; nay, downright pagan instead of Christian sentiments may be sometimes found inscribed in them." Such would be the following, ". . . who possessed by Temper every moral virtue, By religion every Christian Grace . . . In a word few have ever passed a more useful Or a more blameless Life."

With regard to spacing, it is amusing to note the exigencies in which some of the old stonemasons found themselves. It was quite easy in those days to clip a word to make it fit the space, such as the following,

A precious Daughter lieth here
Who was attentive to her parents d
To grieve for her who can refrain
Our loss is her eternal gain.

Considerable local interest should be found in the memorial to Henry Dodd, Brickmaker of Farnham Royal, Bucks, who is described as the "Originator of Annual Sailing Barge Matches – the true School for the Navey, died 1881, aged 80". Our annual efforts, therefore, on the Orwell, must pay tribute to his memory.

Although Suffolk has no stone quarries, this deficiency was made good by those of the Midlands, and one or two local stonemasons have left behind a good record. In West Suffolk the de Carles were responsible for many interior tablets and gravestones throughout that area, during the first half of the nineteenth century. Then, moving nearer home, we have James Pulham, 1765–1830, who worked for William Lockwood, a local (Woodbridge) builder and plasterer at stucco work. About 1816 Lockwood invented an artificial stone, Portland stone cement, and Pulham, along with his brother Obadiah, continued to work for him, later inventing a compound of his own which he named Pulhamite.

James Pulham also worked on tombstones and he has been given the credit for scenes depicting Christ and the Samaritan woman. Most of these examples occur in Suffolk, and it is interesting to note that a headstone to Charles Tooke, 1819, at Wrentham, is adorned with one of these panels, which shows signs of having been let into the surface as a separate tablet. The two figures are grouped about a well-head; Christ is seated beneath a tree, with the woman resting her water-pot on the rim of the well, preparatory to giving Him refreshment. This, together with a replica built into the wall of an alley in Woodbridge, associates it with the name of the local maker of artificial stone, James Pulham, whose tomb is in Woodbridge churchyard. This scene is thought to have appealed because of its everyday country theme.

Another rural emblem, sometimes seen on headstones, and certainly on coats of arms, is the garbe, or wheatsheaf. This calls to mind the old country custom of sending a sheaf of corn to relatives on the death of a farmer.

And whilst on the subject of emblems, there is the 'book', presumably the Bible, An example of this is to be found at St Nicholas's, Ipswich, dated 1790, where a skeleton sits within a coffin holding a book. Then follows the 'hand', with an example at Stoke by Nayland, 1824, where a hand sticking out from clouds, points to a Bible, with this admonition, "Read, Mark, Learn".

Naturally, the macabre creeps in, as at Great Bradley in West Suffolk, where are to be found four coped and coffin-shaped slabs with head and foot stones of the late seventeenth century, two of them with grisly cadavers (skeletons) in bold relief on the ridge. And the unusual, as at Birdbrook, Essex, where there is a tablet in the tower, to Martha Blewett, died 1681. She had nine husbands, and her funeral sermon was preached on the text "Last of all the woman died also".

One of the most interesting cases of survival was to be found at Middleton, near Saxmundham, Suffolk. A former sexton had unearthed a stone ledger, carved with a double omega cross. These slabs are to be found, but are rare. He had an eye to his own end, so he had it cut up to form head and foot stones for his own grave, with the inscription cut on the flat side. The last rector there had it taken into the church, replacing the sexton's memorial with a new one. The omega slab was placed in the chancel. A few years later, when the spire was being repaired, a disastrous fire reduced the church almost to ruins. In clearing away the debris the omega slab disappeared for ever.

The next question is, who wrote these inscriptions? Many of these are to be found dotted up and down the countryside. The village school-master has been given the credit, but in some cases they would almost appear to have come from a book of quotations. For example, a William Hayley was an inveterate writer of epitaphs, and two examples of his verse commemorate parish clerks, then a figure to be found in every village. There were at Eartham in Sussex, Henry Hammond and William Bryant, 1779. The well-known blacksmith epitaph "My sledge and hammer lie reclined, My bellows too have lost their wind", has been attributed to them, although it occurs as early as 1746, at Nettlebed, Oxfordshire. There is an example of this at Darsham, Suffolk. It would be difficult to know how this has travelled over such a wide area.

A very common one, which also appeared on the memorial cards, was:

Afflictions sore long time she bore,
Physicians were in vain.

with variable renderings such as,

Pains were my Portion, Physick was my Food;
Groans were my Devotions; Drugs did me no good;
Christ was my Physician, Knew which way was best,
To relieve me of my Pain, And set my Soul at Rest.

On an old tombstone in Lavenham churchyard was the following:

Every man living
is alltogether vanity,
He heapeth up riches
And cannot tell who shall gather them.

Here lieth the body of John Wills (Batchlor),
late of this Parish
Who departed this life upon the 16th., December
In the year of our Lord 1691
Aged 50 years.

Then comes a Latin inscription, "*Quod fuit esse quod est quod non fuit esse quod esse. Esse quod est non esse, quod non est erit esse.*" Which being interpreted means, more or less –

That which a being was, what is it, show?
That being which it was, it is not now,
To be what 'tis, is not to be, you see;
That which now is not, shall a being be.

This occurs in many places in England.

There was a very good one for the watchmaker:

Here lies in horizontal position
the outside case of
GEORGE ROUTLEIGH, Watchmaker;
Whose abilities in that line were an honour
to his profession,
Integrity was the Mainspring, and prudence the
Regulator,
of all the actions of his life.
Humane, generous and liberal,
His hand never stopped
till he had relieved distress.
So nicely regulated were all his motions,
that he never went wrong,
except when set a-going
by people
who did not know his Key;
even then he was easily
set right again.
He had the art of disposing his time so well,
that his hours glided away
in one continual round
of pleasure and delight,
Until an unlucky minute put a period to
his existence.
He departed this life
Nov. 14,1802:
aged 57:
wound up,

In hopes of being taken in hand
    by his Maker;
And of being thoroughly cleaned, repaired,
    and set a-going
  in the world to come.

And we might end up with one that is to be found in Yoxford churchyard:

The World's a City full of crooked streets;
And Death the Market-place where all men meet;
If Death were merchandise that men could buy,
The rich would always live, the poor must die.

16

Felixstowe Worthies

Oft in the stilly night,
Ere Slumber's chain has bound me,
Fond Memory brings the light
Of other days around me;
The smiles and tears,
Of boyhood's years.

The pictorial parade of Felixstowe has not yet ceased, neither has the photographer's art become dimmed. Every now and again a drawer is turned out, and a sheaf of memories come tumbling about a faded post-card, or a forgotten snap. "Ah, yes, I was younger then, and I do believe that is old so-and-so. Why, he must have been dead and gone these many years. Yes, and that's poor old Annie. Why, she only died last week. How nice and young she do look; bit different to what she grew into. And, I do declare if that isn't Florrie, hurrying off to the grocer's just afore they close. They always did say they could rely on her being the last customer on a Saturday night, although she only lived just round the corner."

Now comes our one great local hero, Field Marshal Lord Allenby, visiting his old home town somewhere after the First World War. He must have had a great affection for Felixstowe, since it figures in his title, second only to the one great battle of Megiddo, that completely routed the Turkish army and drove it out of Palestine. And next to Felixstowe he loved his old mother, Catherine Ann Allenby, to whom he owed so much.

She was one of those forceful characters which the Victorian era produced in such large numbers, such as Catherine Booth, Florence Nightingale and our own Elizabeth Garrett Anderson, the first woman to qualify as a doctor, in this country.

Old Mrs Allenby is still a bright memory in Felixstowe, although she died on 31st October 1922 aged ninety-one, having been a widow for forty-four years. She was particularly known because she drove herself about in a high dog-cart, her coachman Williams (known colloquially as 'Tubby', since he was as broad as long), sitting beside her with folded arms.

It was his mother's forceful personality that gave the Field Marshal his guiding principle through life, a passage out of the Old Book which both loved so much: "Whatsoever thy hand findeth to do, do it with thy might." And it was in Felixstowe that he was able to foster his absorbing love of nature, and garner his great knowledge of birds, flowers and fishes. Here too, it was, where he became skilled in messing about with boats, to wit their 28-ton schooner-rigged yacht, the *Water Witch.*

I have just become possessed of one of old Mrs Allenby's letters, written in a firm and legible hand:

Dec. 2. (1918). Felixstowe House, Felixstowe.

Dear Mrs Harrap

It is very nice to have a letter from you – I remember you as Julia and now in my old age (87 last April) I often think of – and of your father, he used to carry me on his shoulders.

I thank you for your kind congratulations – Genl. Allenby has been wonderfully successful. His great victory at Arras [?] in April 1917 was notable – and he was sent to Egypt in June at three days notice – so that he had not time to bid his son goodbye & the boy 19½ was killed 22 July their only child he had been over a year in the fighting.

When he arriv. in Cairo – the Moslems welcomed him as their deliverer – as they pronounced the name Allenby Allah Nobi, God-The Prophet, as they have a tradition that God would send his Prophet to deliver them – and now his name is mentioned all over the World – since he was chosen to deliver Palestine from the

Turks.

Lady Allenby was allowed to go out to Cairo in October last year & has done good work among the soldiers, & also young officers ever since. The General goes for a few days into Cairo – when he has business to do – it is a ten hour journey he sleeps in the train. I do not know if they are likely to come to England soon – or not.

. . . . I thank you I am in perfect health, but cannot walk, owing to a fall of 3 years ago – when my stick slipped, & let me down – but my sailor son Claude – gave me a wheel chair & I wheel myself in the garden, when fine – & do a bit of weeding, with a garden fork – My 2nd daughter Grace – a widow – lives with me – & my brother John's twin daughter lives in Ipswich & comes to see me. Now good bye –

I am yr. sincerely, C. A. Allenby.

And now a letter from her daughter Grace:

Felixstowe House, Felixstowe, Nov.5th.

Dear Mrs Allenborough

I remember your father Thomas H. quite well & my sister Mrs Andrew tells me to tell you she still has a large wooden linen box which he made & it is always called the Thomas H. box! My mother has been ill for 6 months but has been getting about in her chair till a month ago – & we hoped till the last that her strong vitality would pull her round as it had done so often during this illness. She was unconscious the last 2 days & just quietly passed away in her sleep. She had a very beautiful & happy funeral glorious flowers sent in wreathes & crosses & which we had put in the chancel which was beautifully decorated & the wreathes were put on the grave the next day. The Church packed with people 400 or more [in other words it was full]. The hymns The strife is o'er the battle done, "the 23rd. Psalm & " For ever with the Lord –" & then as she was carried out – "Lord now lettest thou thy servant depart in peace – " It was just what she would have wished – no sadness but a great triumph over death. We are so happy that she is at rest & that she will have regained the use of her limbs – Her brain was clear till the last & her thoughts alwas what she could do for others – I am the daughter Grace mentioned in this letter & I have been a widow for 18 years & shall also be glad when the call comes for me. I am sorry we can't part with the chair it will be kept in the family & is now being lent to an invalid friend & I am sure that is what she would wish.

Believe me yrs. sincerely
(Mrs) Grace Fanshawe

17

Some of our Local Ghosts

And down a narrow lane, well known by day,
With all his speed pursues his sounding way,
In thought still half Absorb'd and chill'd with cold;
When lo! an object frightful to behold;
A grisly Spectre, cloth'd in silver-grey,
Around whose feet the waving shadows play,
Stands in his path. . . .

Robert Bloomfield, "The Farmer's Boy".

Ghosts are numerous in rural England, and have been through all its long history and ghostly past. The Ghost Walk was an alias for some lonely way where you might meet old Tom Shock, one of those former residents of the flesh that seemed to have no wish to depart hence by death, and so returned almost nightly to re-visit old haunts and scenes. These visitants are often related to sudden endings or suicides, suggestion of a broken or incomplete existence. Some act as portents, but these are somewhat impersonal, indefinable appearances. For instance, there was such a visitation at S——, in Church Lane, where a bier-like object was seen by certain people gifted with second sight. But then S—— possessed another and more personal ghost with a quite beneficent turn of mind, to wit an old workman, who came nightly to one of the old twine-spinning and rope-making sheds then standing, and did a shift of work.

Then a wraithe-like object could sometimes be seen at C——, but this pursued an aimless existence; while a house at A——

held some quite unpleasant spirits that gave the occupants a very bad time, brushing rudely past them on the stairs, and behaving generally in a rude and boisterous manner. Many of the portent variety, especially in coastal areas were understood as premonitions of loss of life by shipwreck; incidents all too common at one time.

In fact one might say almost every village had its ghosts, and they became so numerous that ghostly counsel had to be sought and these unreasonable apparitions 'laid' and read into order. Part of the formula was, "In the name of the Father, Son and Holy Ghost, what troubleth thee?" Ingredients of the cure have been discovered in a large Bible, a whip, glass, gloves and a bridle. But not every parson had the gift, or was equal in power.

The Red Stile at W—— was a rare place to see a ghost; shroud-like in white, or white with black about the head. One night a fellow was coming along the D—— road with a friend of his, when he suddenly saw his old grandmother – dead long since – sitting on that same stile. He was so taken aback that he must needs go up and touch her; but perhaps you know that you must not try to touch a ghost. She 'whooly' scared him, so that he began to run away, but she up and caught him, twisted him round three times until he fell plump in the 'holl'.

"What are yew a-running for like that, partner?" exclaimed his mate. He was all of a muck sweat, dripping from his face. And the side of his body where his old grandmother had touched him was numb!

"But thare, Bor! a good many fooks hev bin regular thrown aback a passing thet owd Red Stile."

And that was not the only ghost to be found in W——, for a young man who worked at L—— was also 'whooly' scared and trembled from head to foot, by 'suffen' that stood in the hedge close by an old elm tree on the road from M—— to L——. He was so afraid that his old father had to come each night and help him past the spot.

Perhaps it was the same spirit that haunted the road near B——, and was seen by a woman on her way to make a call. She soon scuttled off home and waited until it got light.

And, of course, it was not always nice to have a house with a garden that backed on to the churchyard. For sometimes, when you could not sleep, you could hear your china – if you had any – chinking about at midnight as though it was being got ready for a meal. And you did not feel comfortable about it, but you did not do anything, for it is advisable to give ghosts plenty of room.

The L—— road was another favourite haunt for ghostly visitors, especially the bit by the Mount – still to be seen – hidden in the hedge. If you were driving along here in a pony cart, it was no uncommon sensation to realize that 'something' was driving after you, and if you got the old mare to go a bit faster, as well you might, so 'that' would follow faster. But 'it' would never catch you up!

A man and a woman once walking along here saw something in the road, and the man being stupid 'lumped his owd stick into it!' When lo! he was suddenly whisked over the hedge, taken several yards into the field. And then brought back to continue his walk by his wife, a sadder and wiser man.

If you were born in the chime hours, you could hear music in the ruins of the old abbey, but if you went to investigate, the music stopped, to resume again as you drew away. But you must keep out of the secret passage that runs from here to F—— for if you do go in you may never come out again – like so many others who have never been seen since!

And yet there have been ghosts of flesh and blood, as seen by two boys over at Y——. They saw 'it' moving, and being less scared than some crept nearer and nearer to hear it mumbling to itself. But alas and alack, it was only poor old Pernina Marjoram, out in her night shift when she should have been abed. As everyone knew, she was not quite normal.

It is therefore hardly to be wondered at that we have, or had, a ghost in our village, which was seen within quite recent times. It haunts and frequents that house of some pretensions that stands at the acute bend of the road as you go by the ancient causeway or 'carnser'. For long now it has been the home, albeit altered and added to, of an old artist of gentle mien. His hands are stiffened now and his feet painfully calloused, where once they were supple and nimble. Yet he holds in his eyes secret beauties of our locality that he has seen and known, whereas we passed all unheedingly. Some he has transferred to canvas, and some will pass over when his senses change. And when not painting or preparing his canvases, some of which have cracked because he wrought too quick upon them, he has cultivated a living art – the propagation of irises. He knows every bloom in that little corner of his garden, marrying this one to that and producing rare and lovely colours, and then giving them a name. And the question remains unanswered – which art is the greater?

His home is an interesting collection of old and new in houses, once a farmhouse holding plenty of oak beams and leaded windows, capped by a creeping shingle-tiled roof. This, the old portion, but it has been added to and enlarged in an Italianesque style to suit the requirements of our old friend and his family. In the old part you will find as nice a floor of old sweet chestnut; boards some 15 ins to 18 ins wide; as in a long search, shining now as they have not shone for many a long year, fastened with old cut-head nails of local blacksmith make. The rooms ramble about as country rooms do, and if you go through that little doorway into the apartment over the kitchen, which was an old dairy, you may notice, if you look carefully, the flail marks in the sloping ceiling, evidence of the half stick used to thrash out a little corn, or maybe some seed.

But if the old place has been altered beyond recognition and you have to look long to see the old portion, settling in amid the new, yet it has not lost its old character, for it is haunted. It happened long years ago now, when an old doctor came here to live a retired and quiet life. Of kindly intent, he doctored the village folk without regard to fees, and did what good he could. Presently he tired of the old house, why no one could tell, and built himself a brand new, square-faced, box-of-bricks pattern, just

11 Lowestoft Church

12 Bridge Street, Great Glemham

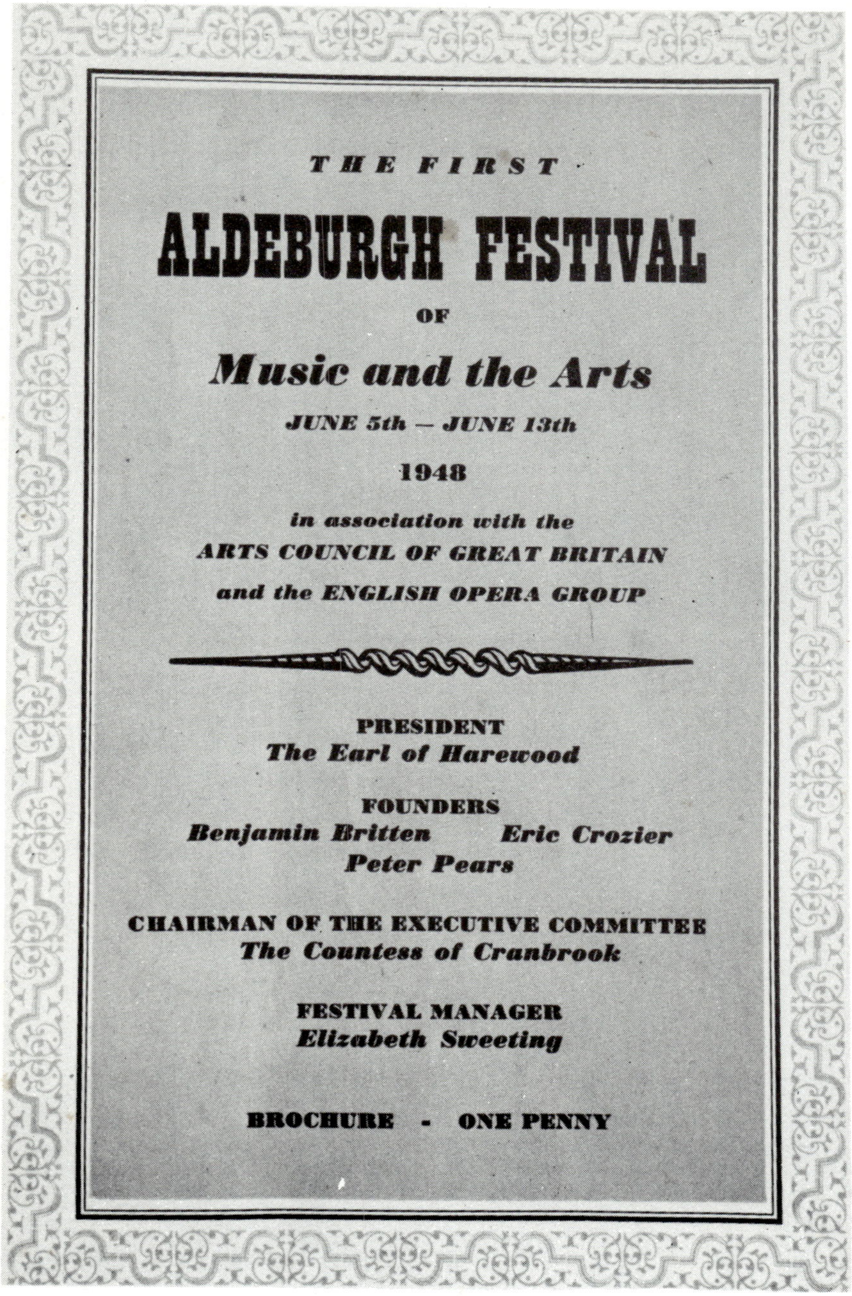
THE FIRST

ALDEBURGH FESTIVAL

OF

Music and the Arts

JUNE 5th — JUNE 13th

1948

in association with the

ARTS COUNCIL OF GREAT BRITAIN

and the ENGLISH OPERA GROUP

PRESIDENT

The Earl of Harewood

FOUNDERS

Benjamin Britten *Eric Crozier*

Peter Pears

CHAIRMAN OF THE EXECUTIVE COMMITTEE

The Countess of Cranbrook

FESTIVAL MANAGER

Elizabeth Sweeting

BROCHURE - ONE PENNY

13 Brochure for the first Aldeburgh Festival in 1948

across the way. A regular money-box-looking affair, that simply stands and stares across the marshes from under its thatched-hat. And yet, in time, the old man grew tired even of this, and one day he was found in the pond, under the hedge, within a stone's throw of his first love. They buried him in the churchyard at dead of night, as befitted suicides, but that was not the end. And sometimes, to those born in the chime hours, he can still be seen, not in the money-box house, but in the old portion of the old house, where memories and flail marks linger, and old floorboards creak and timbers groan.

You will not find him in the studio, a fine large hall in the new wing, where hang triumphs of other years in Academy trophies, but in the old room now a dining place. He sits pensive in a chair, and the daughter of the house knows him quite well. They do say that if you make a rustling noise, sibilant like old silk, he looks up with a strangely bright interested look, and moves involuntarily to meet the sound. Can it be that tragedy waits eternally on time and finds no solution, even in desperate remedies?

"He is here again Nigel," she would say to her brother, "in the same spot and the same chair!" And Nigel could see him too; and they would go gently lest he should be disturbed. But the reverend seniors could not see, neither knew of his presence, as it was a secret between these two. Obviously he was attached to his old home, and maybe regretted the rash act that sent his body to our green acre that could not hold his spirit nor be his rest. Perhaps he waits for patients who now need him not having been cured by that ground sweat that settles so many disorders.

No Will-o-th'-Wisp mislight thee;
Nor snake, or slow-worm bite thee;
    But on, on thy way
    Not making a stay,
Since ghosts there's none to affright thee.

Herrick

18

Cures by Magic and Folk Medicine

Here's Penny Royal and Marigolds,
Come buy my misteltoe,
Come buy my wormwood and mugwort,
Here's all fine herbs of every sort,
Here's southernwood that's very good,
Dandelion and houseleek,
Here's dragon's tongue and wood sorrell,
With bear's foot and horehound.

When old soldiers of the First World War paid a visit to the doctor's for necessitous or base ends it was almost universally known as reporting to the quack. True, such a visit might end in medicine and duty, but quack was the doctor's cognomen, be he never so capable. It was an old army term dating back to the early days of medicine when old wives culled their remedies from the hedgerows.

It has been suggested that it might be derived from the East Anglian 'quake' doctors who treated malaria in the marshlands of that area until the late eighteenth century. The trouble could be charmed away by pinning a lock of hair to an aspen tree and chanting, "Aspen Tree, Aspen tree, I prithee to shake and shiver of me". Certainly the term covered a multitude of charlatans, sinners and fortune hunters.

But of one thing we may be sure, that whereas the quacks may have been given to sharp practices, your wise woman (sometimes a man), did her or his beneficent work, not only in an enjoined silence, but for no monetary gain.

First of all the person to be operated upon comes to the curer with a full and earnest belief that the cure will be efficacious. Secondly that the words 'please' or 'thank you', do not occur during the process. The established formula consists of the charmer crossing the part affected and whispering over it mysterious words.

The quack used both eyes and hands as instruments of diagnosis and usually his conclusions were correct.

James Murrell, nicknamed the cunning man of Hadleigh, Essex, belonged to the class of village wise-men. He treated both human beings and animals – the former by herbal medicines and the latter by sound veterinary skill, plus a little magic. His living-room was festooned with drying herbs. In his treatment of the emotionally disturbed his role was little more than that of a witch doctor, driving out the demons of disease by exorcism, reinforced by specially made iron 'witch bottles', these being standard equipment for the magician. The bottles were filled with blood and urine taken from the patient and were then brought to the boil on the kitchen stove, while the Lord's Prayer was recited backwards.

Within ten miles of Murrell lived Thomas Bedloe of Rawreth, known as the 'Cancer Quack'. A board outside his cottage bore the sign, "Thomas Bedloe, hog, dog and cattle doctor. Immediate relief and perfect cure for persons in the dropsy, also eating cancer."

Known also as the 'Dropsy Doctor', Bedloe was consulted by clients for miles around. He was extremely skilled at herbal cures and for the treatment of the 'quakes', the malarial plague of Essex marshlands.

Yet another was Old Dido, the medical herbalist of Epping Forest, who not only prepared his own remedies but cared for the sick patients skilfully, and usually free of charge.

It is only of recent years that the power of suggestion has been given scientific merit in psychology, and for long enough the power of the royal touch by which scrofula sufferers found relief by faith in physical contact has been systematized in the art of psychiatry. Queen Anne was the last of the British monarchs to exercise this cure. This was carried to excess when many scofulus persons continued to make pilgrimage to Ashburnham Church, Sussex, for the purpose of touching a pair of drawers and shirt worn by Charles I, in the hope of a miraculous cure.

I have read Eric Maple's *Magic, Medicine and Quackery* with the greatest interest, because Suffolk like all other rural areas was steeped in this sort of thing. It must be realized that doctors were amongst the most primitive of professional men in their knowledge and skill. This was witnessed by Constable the painter, writing from Hampstead in 1827. "I find medical men knew nothing of this terrible disorder (whooping cough) and can afford no relief; consequently it is in the hands of quacks. I have been advised to put him [his little son] three times over and under a donkey as a perfect cure." That doctors were few in number and hard to come by in time of need, threw folks on their own resources and methods of care and attention. Even surgery was more a matter of expediting death rather than effecting a cure.

Egypt appears to have been the birthplace of medical science and their greatest physician Imhotep was elevated to the status of a god after his death. Their knowledge was revealed by the discovery of the Ebers papyrus in a tomb in Luxor. This consisted of a comprehensive set of medical prescriptions and methods of treatment. Eric Maple points out that much of this vast knowledge was attained by the embalmers, who were employed in the 'House of the Dead', in removing organs from bodies. During the centuries the anatomical secrets of the human frame came under observation, with the result that they had a greater knowledge of physiology in those far off days than existed in the eighteenth century.

Walter Budge in his *Egyptian Magic* said: "The Egyptian in common with many other Eastern nations believed that certain sicknesses and diseases might be cured by certain medicaments pure and simple, but that others needed not only drugs but words of power to effect their cure." For example the ancient oculist applying an ointment would utter these words, "Come ointment, come: come thou verdant oil". These were none other than the words uttered in the old farmhouse dairies when churning:

Come, butter come,
Peter stands at the gate
Waiting for a buttered cake,
Come, butter, come.

Arising directly from the process of embalming the art of bandaging came into the world, while Egyptian hygiene principles exerted a profound influence upon the sanitary laws of first the Jews and later on all mankind. Blood letting was as familiar to the Egyptians as to the physicians of medieval Europe.

To the Greeks belongs the Hippocratic oath, as also that comprehensive medical theory, the principle of contraries: "To cool what is hot, to warm what is cold, to dry what is moist, to moisten what is dry". And it was Aesculapius who became the god of medicine and healing.

It would appear that the Church took over from the pagan faiths. The medieval holy wells derived from the old worship of wells and springs, and these developed into the spa. These wells are common to Suffolk where ever a religious house found a habitation. There was probably one in Felixstowe where I live. Certainly Brightwell provides an example. They were usually considered beneficial for ophthalmic trouble. Spas were alleged to cure apoplexy, epilepsy, catalepsy and vertigo; cleared the stomach, opened the lungs and abolished asthma and scurvy, black and yellow jaundice, hypochondria, windiness and melancholy.

A famous well was that of Clerkenwell, London, that bore the notice: "A.D. 1800 Willm Bound, Joseph Bird, Churchwardens. For the better accommodation of the Neighbourhood, this Pump was removed to the spot where it now stands. The Spring by which it is supplied is situated four feet eastward, and round it, as history informs us, the Parish Clerks of London in remote Ages annually performed sacred Plays. That custom caused it to be denominated Clerks Well, and from which this Parish derives its name. The Water was greatly esteemed by the Prior and Brethren of the Order of St John of Jerusalem, and the Benedictine Nuns of the neighbourhood."

The waters of Walsingham were extremely popular among those with stomach disorders. At St Tegia's Well, Denbighshire, the sick pilgrims were required to encircle the waters three times and lay fourpence upon the shrine. There was a well at Dunwich near the Lazar Chapel, now lost sight of, the water of which was stone cold on the hottest day and where in later days the village women did their washing.

The influence of the Church is also seen in the incantations which accompanied healing by touch, such as those used by burn-curers:

> There were three Angels came from the North,
> One brought fire, the other brought frost;
> Come out fire, go in frost.
> Father, Son and Holy Ghost.

This association with the Church reminds us that the ague was alleviated if a ring made from coffin handles could be worn. Amulets also played a part, consisting of pieces of parchment on which passages of the Gospels had been inscribed.

The monks were undoubtedly acquainted with the old Anglo-Saxon herbals and knew the secrets of the hedgerows and the healing virtues of henbane, camomile, horehound, fennel, mustard, rosemary, celandine, wormwood, hellebore and many others. Liverwort was used to alleviate disorders of that organ, and eye-bright cured optical diseases. Snakebite was treated with Viper's bugloss, and yellow elderberry provided a cure for yellow jaundice. Herbal lore with its magical symbolism was of immense significance in the home, but the plant, to be effective, had to be gathered at the appropriate time and season.

This is brought out in *The Leopard* by Giuseppe di Lampedusa, when describing an evening party, "The only one to stay with us was the herbalist who would not be going to bed that night as there was a new moon and he had to gather rosemary on the Pietrazzi rocks. . . . He had an understanding of the old anti-catarrhal laxative, and even aphrodisiac properties of his herbs."

For asthma one drank wine in which wood lice had been steeped, and for loss of memory the forehead was rubbed with castor oil. Cramp could be cured by a garter made from rosemary leaves or eelskin, and sore eyes healed by powdered hens' dung. And was it not a secret remedy of a Shropshire woman in 1775 that led to the discovery of digitalis for the heart affections and as a cure for dropsy?

However, it was generally conceded that old wives, gypsies, masters of the black art, old peasant folks, had more knowledge of such things than all the colleges and universities put together. Moreover, cures were more efficacious if administered by the seventh child of a seventh child.

When George Crabbe, our Aldeburgh Poet, commenced to practise medicine the local folk noticed he got his medicines from the wild herbs growing thereabouts. They were of the opinion that as he obtained them for nothing, he had no need of payment.

John Wesley compiled a manual of *Primitive Physic*, which contains nearly 300 remedies. Many of them are marked as having been tried, but some would be expensive to administer today, such as, "The Itch: wash the parts affected with strong rum – Tried." "Legs, Sore and Runnings: Wash them in brandy and apply elder leaves, changing twice a day. Or poultice them with rotten apples, Tried."

Then come the following. "A Strong Purge: drink half a pint of strong decoction of dock root." "For Asthma: live for a fortnight on boiled carrots only. It seldom fails." "A Cold in the Head: pare very thin the yellow rind of an orange. Roll it up inside out, and thrust a roll in each nostril." "Consumption: in the last stage, suck a healthy woman daily. This cured my father."

It is interesting to know that Daffay's elixir for flatulence came from a still at Dawes Heath, Thundersly, in Essex, an area noted for medicinal herbs. But it was Francis Moore, schoolmaster, physician and astrologer, who launched the almanacs that still bear his name, to advertise his oils, the secrets of which have been lost.

One of the most colourful of the quacks was Sequah, of Red-Indian fame. It appears there was a long line of these and the last died in the 1920s in England. These men practised at fairs, and would arrive in a smart little buggy drawn by a pair of spanking ponies. The *modus operandi* was to gather a crowd, offer to take out teeth painlessly (the screams of the victim being drowned by a band of music), and to cure all kinds of lameness. A person so afflicted would have his crutch snapped across Sequah's knee, and be sent away rejoicing. Alas, the cure would wear itself out in a day or so and the lame one find himself in bad need of his crutch.

James Hallett was a well-known Sussex quack who flourished at the latter end of the seventeenth century. His handbill is worth reciting.

GREAT NEWS TO THE AFFLICTED! To all who are afflicted with diseases, let them be ever so stubborn or long standing, or if given up by physicians, or turned out of hospitals incurable shall with the help of God be radically cured by James Hallett, the original curer of all diseases.

Cancers, King's Evil, scrofula and scorbutic eruptions, sore heads, scald heads, deafness and roaring noises in the head, blindness and bad eyes, diseases of the head, brains and nerves, palsy, apoplexy, lethargy, convulsions, frenzy, vertigo, inveterate headache, deplorable nervous distempers, melancholy in men and vapours in women, bilious cases, debility, indigestion, cough and colds, lowness of spirits, loss of appetite, all impurity of the blood, relaxation, rheumatic and other gouts, yellow red and other jaundice agues, asthma and all diseases of the lungs, exulcerated lungs and livers, strengthens the liver, the memory made good, white swelling in the knee, St Anthony's fire, St Vitus's dance, corns either hard or soft and a certain disease whether fresh or thirty years standing. Cured by herbs only, wens of all sizes and all other diseases of tedious tormentation, cured by James Hallett, the original curer of all diseases.

He may be seen at his new house three doors from the Waggon and Lamb, West-Gate, Chichester, every Wednesday and Thursday until 10, and Saturday until 3 o'clock. To be seen at No 8 Halfway-house on Saturday evening, Sunday, Monday and Tuesday, until 11 o'clock.

A universal ointment for the chilblains and chap hands, that will cure them in a few hours, if not broke, and another ointment that will soon cure them if broke.

Surely a pretty wide range and one wonders how old he was when he came to his end. With such skill of diagnosis and prescription one might live for ever.

19

Yesterday's Advertisements

Blest be the man, whose happy skill
Avails to lessen human ill;
And be his brow with honours crown'd;
He merits well the glorious palm,
Who first with eye sagacious found
That greatest blessing – Gilead's Balm.

Advertising as we know it to-day, and which to a large extent governs our lives, is comparatively modern. I am old enough to remember when such things were bald and unconvincing, and of a very limited type. We lived near a railway station in south-east London, and the placards announced such things as "Hudson's Soap", the two words caught in the rays of a hand lamp; or "Stephen's Ink", scrawled across a huge blot of that liquid (the sort of thing that illuminated my copybook at school); and a famous pen, or nib, bearing the refrain, "The Pickwick, the Owl and the Waverley Pen,/Come as a boon and a blessing to Men". Then there was "Monkey Brand Soap", with the proviso, "It won't wash Clothes", illustrated by a monkey using a scoured frying pan as a mirror. The most fetching example was the famous picture, entitled "Bubbles", painted by Sir John Everett Millais and used by Pears' Soap.

In due time the baldness was enlivened by the famous *Punch* picture of the tramp writing his testimonial (always unsolicited in those days): "Dear Sir; Ten years ago I used your soap, since when I have used no other."

Advertising as such, commenced somewhere about the beginning of the eighteenth century, and it is interesting to note that it was the quacks who started it. Since doctors, in too many cases, were the merest charlatans, this is not surprising. Daffy's Elixir became famous by this means, claiming its wonderful effects on all complaints. In 1735, this panacea could be obtained in Ipswich at Bagnall's Printing Office; Mr Raff's, grocer, in the Butter Market; Mr Hudson, grocer, in the Corn Hill; and of Mr Bedwell at the Spotted Horse in St Nicholas's. These and other advertisements mentioned here are taken from "Suffolk Notes", appearing in the *Ipswich Journal*.

Then followed Mr James Thirn, clock maker, Woodbridge; Mr Andrews, barber, Saxmundham; Mr Butcher in Yoxford; Mr Chinnery in Needham Market, Mr Atkinson in Stowmarket; Mr Mathias Berry in Framlingham; and by Charles Fox, the newsman at Ufford.

At this time too Thomas Warner, a horse and cow leech at Woodbridge, advertised a "Milch Ass, with a *fole* by her side, to let". This was evidently for asses' milk, much regarded until mid-Victorian times.

In those days, 1804, proprietary medicines, as they were called, were in full flourish, and Dr Steer's 'Opoldeldock' was on the market, together with Newbery's Pectoral Essence of Coltsfoot, Dr Brodum's Syrup and the Cordial Balm of Gilead. This latter was evidently designed for the religious cottager, who would be misled into thinking that he or she was being offered some biblical remedy. Then there were Gall's Antibilious Pills, and the Messrs Newbery gave a long list of their particular specialities.

An advertisement appeared in 1764 which has a modern flavour about it in this Welfare State, it reads:

> Tincture of Sage. A new and Noble Medicine, for preventing the Decays of Age, and lengthening Human Life. Invented by Dr Hill and now first published.
>
> It continues Health and Spirits to the Extream [sic] of Life,

preserves the Faculties and Memory, warms the Heart, strengthens the Stomach and restores lost appetite. A pleasant, innocent, and most effectual Medicine, refreshing, cheery and enlivening. A gentle Glow, the genuine Warmth of Youth, spreads gradually through the body, upon taking it, the whole Frame becomes alert, and more alive, the Breath is easy, and the Limbs are free and pliant; the Head is clear and undisturbed, and Heart light and jovial. It prevents disorders from a sedentary habit, and relieves instantly in Faintings, Tremblings, and every kind of Discomposure. It is useful to those who are to speak in Public, fortyfying the mind against the Terrors of an Audience and at once composing the Thoughts and enlivening the Imagination.

What a panacea this must have been! But I do not think it would have taken in my old grandfather or any of his forebears. These advertisers seemed to be all doctors and as there was no Register, they could not have been struck off.

This same year a German physician living at Bury attacked a Chevallier Taylor, oculist, by inserting an advertisement in which he doubted the supposed cures by the Chevallier, and challenged him to produce the original testimonials. The advertisement was unique in its way.

To the Chevallier Taylor, Oculist, to all the Crowned Heads (except the King of Prussia, whose eyes, I hope never want couching) Author of above forty Volumes.

Sir, I shall be glad to be acquainted with the celebrated Dr Child of Lavenham (ten miles from Bury) above 80 years of age and according to the Certificate of the noted Surgeon, Mr J. Thomas of Lavenham mentioned in his letter dated May 5 in the *Ipswich Journal* of May the 12th, the above Dr Child, after being five years entirely deprived of Sight, he was on Thursday last, the 3rd, restored by the Hands etc, could discern any objects? Whether it continued to this very day? It is my humble opinion if Dr Child is really restored to Sight he must be able to discern many objects one from another, or else he cannot be said to be restored to Sight etc.

The Chevallier will oblige me very much and without doubt many others of the Faculty to give us a catalogue of the Forty

Volumes written by himself in different Parts of the World, in what Language they were published and of whom to be had. As I am a Prussian and studied many Years in one of his Majestie's Universities (Duisberg on the Rhine) and afterwards at Leyden, Utrecht and Harderwyck, I expect the Chevallier's answer in the next *Ipswich Journal* either in Greek or Latin, High German or Low Dutch, and opposite the Translation in English. I am, Sir

Your humble Servant,

May 23, 1764 Peter Van Sarn, M.D., at Bury St Edmunds

This appears to me rather childish, I understand there was no answer.

Twenty years later appears a notice concerning a learned treatise on a disease which is still a recurring affliction with us: "A work has just been published by R. Hamilton, M.D. Physician in Ipswich, containing a description of the influenza as it appeared in Hertfordshire and Bedfordshire, Spring 1742, with its Distinctions and Methods of Cure." The same author also published a pamphlet of "Thoughts for the Establishement of a Regimental Fund for the relief of Sick Wives of the Soldiery, and Hints relative to Marriages among Privates".

And here is something which was formerly highly esteemed amongst invalids. "Spruce Beer being now the fashionable drink at all polite places and even in assemblies, as a substitute for Negus, to enable every person to have the wholesome and cheap liquor, an Essence is now prepared and sold by J. Shave of Ipswich, in pots at 9s. each which will make 63 gallons, at 5s. pot 30 gallons, and at 3s. 6d. pot 20 gallons. To such as are forbid the use of malt liquors this is a valuable acquisition."

Whilst on this subject, it might be noted that for the week-ending 13th December 1729 appears this: "To be sold to the best bidder, a Public House at Eyke, known as the Sign of the Castle, together with a Barn, Stable Yards, Garden and Orchard, with about 10 acres of land, and Right of Commonage, worth about four pounds per annum. Enquire of Mr Thomas Long at Melton or of Mr John Fuller at Eyke."

This, of course, was when innkeepers were also farmers, or had other occupations besides the selling of beer, the latter being often the perquisite of the wife. However, the following appeared under 1730:

Bacchus turned honest, or good advice to Tipplers. My Friend,

If you would have good wine, and a great deal of respect in a Tavern, use it but seldom, and be sure pay ready money, or suffer your name to sully but one page of their bar book, it makes the Master familiar, and the drawer saucy; Besides it is a certain maxim in their politics to impose upon their best customers, and always to treat them with the greatest respect that are their smallest benefactors, for the devil and most vintners are of one temper, and will not be industrious to oblige the person they are sure of.

Repenting fools have oft confest
That thriving Vintners make lean Guests;
As they grow rich there's nothing surer
Than that you Topers prove the poorer;
Therefore when'er they're saucy grown
Complain not, for the Fault's your own;
'Tis nonsense at their pride to grumble,
Since you yourselves may keep them humble;
Spend warily, and you will find
Yourselves more happy, them more kind.

In 1764 the Bath Houses in Aldeburgh were advertised, and mention was made of the invention of a bathing machine, which was thus described. "And for the conveniency of those Bathing in the Real Ocean, there is a curious machine, that by the assistance of a single person may be run into the sea to any depth proper for bathing." It was many years before such a thing appeared on our beaches at Felixstowe.

Agriculture took its turn as the machine age came in, and we get this in 1803:

Threshing Machines
Manufactured by Wm. Dixon & Co.
Ipswich.

W. Dixon (from Durham), having had fourteen years experience in the manufacture of the above machines, which have met with general approbation think it the less necessary to say much in their behalf by a printed advertisement, but refers to Robert Ransome, Iron Founder, Ipswich, for such particulars as may be required, where orders are received for them, and for Winnowing Machines, Chaff Engines, Bean Mills, etc.

The next year, 1804, Mr Jacob Garrett, of the New Foundry, Ipswich, announced his intention to temper his cast-iron shares according to the soil they were intended for, for which he charged 12s. per dozen. S. Garrett of Farnham, also generously offered to serve the eastern part of Suffolk for his brother, at whose shop old iron would be taken on the same terms as at the foundry. A significant postscript, showing the steadiness of the times, is attached to this advertisement. "N.B. No person may expect so large an order as 80 doz. to be executed at once, as the general satisfaction anyhow given, has always prevented that accumulation."

It appears that moveable folds for sheep were introduced about this time by Mr Plowman of Brome, near Eye, who first exhibited them at Lord Somerville's Cattle Show.

Mr Plowman exhibited the model of a portable fold for sheep, in which by means of small wheels, a whole side can be moved, or even the whole fold shoved upon fresh ground daily without taking it to pieces. It was said that Mr Plowman had had the fold for more than two years to use. It appeared also that a slight alteration in the construction of this useful fold, and making it stronger and heavier, would enable the farmer to pen hogs upon his clover, tares, or any other green crop, which is a great *desideratum* in agriculture.

This brings us to wagers, and trials of skill in woodland crafts. The first comes from Framlingham in 1743:

Gentlemen. This is to let you know from me, William Alexander, Lath and Pale Cleaver in Framlingham, in the County of Suffolk, that I will make a Wager for Five Pounds Sterling with any one Lath Cleaver, in the County aforesaid, that I do make as much of a load of oaken rift into lath, and the lath as good, by the judgement of three men that understand it, where there are two lengths of a tree, I will make one, and the other, and so on, let the timber be great or small or twisted.

This was answered by one from Woodbridge:

This is to give notice to all gentlemen and others, that I, William Miret, Lath Render, of Woodbridge, do challenge William Alexander, of Framlingham, to reave forty feet of timber; and to try which of us can make most laths, and best and quickest, by the judgement of two men, for five pounds, a Half Crown Bowl of Punch, or a crooked pin. William Hirst.

Whether the trial of skill ever took place one can never know. It seems to have closed in a vein of sarcasm. But the challenge continued.

Whereas John and William Alexander, of Framlingham, have twice advertised themselves in the Ipswich Journal to cleave laths of Pale with any other man in the County for Five Pounds: I William Miret of Woodbridge, have let them know by advertisement and by several letters that I have sent them, that I will work with them as they propose for Five Pounds, either at Framlingham or Woodbridge.

The excuse William Alexander made was that he would work any where else excepting Framlingham and Woodbridge.

This is further to let him know, as his dislike is to these places, I will get 40 feet of timber carried to Melton, and if he or his brother John will meet me there to work, I will give him or his brother their board during the time of working, or will meet him within a mile of Framlingham, or where else, if he will find timber.

N.B. If one or both of these bragging gentlemen have since had a thought that they are deficient in any part of their trade, I will send my little prentice boy over to instruct them.

Now comes something under date of 1824 concerning an old firm that is still with us, now under the name of Debenhams:

JUST ARRIVED
And will be open and ready for Inspection
This day, the 3rd of July,
At Waterloo House,
Butter Market, Ipswich.

The largest and best assortment of Linen and Woollen Drapery ever before offered to the Public. – A part of this immense stock consists of about 400 pieces of yard-and-a-half wide cambric muslin at Threepence halfpenny per yard; a large quantity of foreign nankeen, 5 yard lengths at 2s. 8d. per piece; some very superior ditto, warranted 9 yards at 30s. 6d. per piece; also about 100 pieces of calico at 1½d. per yard; some very stout ditto at 3½d. and about 700 pieces of very superior shirtings at 6d. which

FOOTMAN AND CO

Can warrant to be made of the very best materials, and for strength and durability cannot be equalled by any House in the Kingdom.

There is no indication of a queue being formed or that goods cannot be taken out of the windows until the morning of the sale.

We might end our catalogue with the rather unique announcement:

TO ALL GENTLEMEN CRICKETERS

This is to give notice that on Tuesday next, the 31st instant [1784] will be given gratis by Thomas Podd, at his Grand Hotel Booth on Ipswich Race-Ground, Eleven pair of doe-skin Gloves to any eleven men who shall play for and win the same, at the noble and manly game of Cricket according to the rules and orders of the game. It is hoped that the gentlemen who would wish to try their skill and dexterity at the above game will be on the ground by one o'clock, as a cold collation will be provided by their humble servant. T. Podd.

20

Ipswich Reflections

A recent announcement in the Press (September, 1978), stated that a 1611 map of Suffolk by the British cartographer John Steed, which contains a plan of Ipswich, fetched £230.

It is a very interesting study to trace some of the street names of old Ipswich; they cluster about the dock area. I give their map reference to show their close proximity. One wonder, for instance the significance of Dial Lane (E5). Coprolite Street (E5), reminds us of the discovery of these fossilized excrements discovered in Suffolk in the late eighteenth century and evidently shipped from Ipswich to the experimental station at Rothamsted, or sent up the river to Stowmarket. Holywells (F6), speaks for itself of curative water greatly esteemed before the Reformation. Key Street (E5) – this is obviously an old rendering of 'Quay'. Rope Walk (E5) tells of the great shipbuilding years as far back as Tudor times, when the great cables were made of cords tightly interwoven. Ship Launch Road (E6) speaks of great events, and as large a vessel as could be got down the Orwell. Silent Street (D5) must surely refer to old monkish times, or was it a very quiet and select thoroughfare?

This brings us to Lady Lane (D5), and this is what G. R. Clarke has to say about it in his *History of Ipswich*, published in May 1830:

> St Mary's chapel, commonly called *Our Lady of Grace* stood at the N.W. corner of the lane, without the gate, which to this day goes by the name of Lady Lane. This chapel was famous for an image of the

Blessed Virgin, much resorted to and to which, in old wills, many pilgrimages were ordered to be made; and it was styled Our Lady of Ipswich. This venerated image shared the fate of other relics of superstition; for it was conveyed to London, and publicly burned. The site of the chapel is now covered with buildings.

It was to this chapel that Cardinal Wolsey ordered an annual procession to be made by the dean of his college, on 8th September, being the nativity of the Virgin Mary, the tutelary saint of Ipswich; and no doubt the benign influence of this guardian saint of the town has had its due effect upon the chastity and virtue of the highly-favoured inhabitants. In Grove's *Dialogue between Wolsey and Cardinal Ximenes*, published in 1761, is a plan of the streets through which the procession passed. The image of Our Lady of Ipswich is mentioned as a notorious object of idolatry in the homilies of the Church of England. It must have been a religious house of note at an early period of our history; for an old MS mentions – upon what authority we know not – that in the year 1297, Elizabeth, the daughter of Edward I, was married to John, Count of Holland, at the Chapel of Our Lady of Ipswich.

In the year 1515, Mr Edmund Daundy erected fifteen alms'-houses now standing in Lady Lane, for the poor of the parish, and gave by his will, wood to each of his alms'-houses "besides Our Lady of Grace"; but the revenue for the support of these houses, is lost.

The Guild of Our Lady of Ipswich has been revived, and a Pilgrimage Walk was held on Thursday, 7th September 1978, commemorating and celebrating the procession ordered by His Grace, Cardinal Wolsey, which took place on the same day in 1528, Our Lady's Eve. Here follows the itinerary:

St Peter's Church, mentioned in Domesday Book. Served as Chapel for Wolsey's College.

The Wolsey Gate. Only remains here of the College of Secular Canons dedicated to the Virgin.

Star Lane. To St Mary Quay Church which was originally Our Lady Star of the Sea.

St Peter's Street. Many sixteenth- and seventeenth-century

buildings between nos 11 and 13, opening, leads to courtyard, possibly earlier with oriel windows.

Silent Street. Both Henry VIII and Catherine of Aragon stayed here when visiting the Shrine.

St Nicholas' Church. Mainly fourteenth-century and fifteenth-century on the site of earlier St Michael's.

Queen Street. Carmelite Friary extended from Queen Street to St Stephen's Lane in 1278.

Cornhill. Westgate Street. Had many Inns used by Pilgrims. West Gate. The West or Bur Gate of the town was at the end of Westgate Street. It contained the Common Gaol and was pulled down in 1782. Joining it on each side were the town walls.

Lady Lane. Here was the Chapel of Our Lady of Grace. Nothing is left today, but we know that it stood back from the lane, had a burial ground, a porch, stained-glass windows, and was large enough to hold more than sixty people. It contained a statue of the Madonna that was nationally famed, was visited by countless Pilgrims and, even though alleged to have been destroyed in 1538, is believed to be still revered in Nettuno in Italy.

The Shrine of Our Lady of Grace stood in Lady Lane, Ipswich, from at least 1297 to 1538. It contained a famed statue of the Blessed Virgin Mary and was a place of regular Pilgrimage. The untold number of people who came in thanksgiving or supplication had among them noted personalities, including royalty. It is one of the aims of the Guild of Our Lady of Ipswich that the town shall again become a centre of devotion to the Mother of God.

When Cardinal Wolsey built his Ipswich College he ordered an annual procession to the Shrine. Only one took place, but an old and rare book tells of the route and those taking part. These included the College staff of Dean, Sub-Dean, six Priests, eight Clerics, nine Choristers, all their servants, the Priors of Christ Church and Butley, the Vicar of Aldborough, some personal friends of his Grace, the Bailiffs and Portmen of Ipswich and 'most of the Gentlemen of the County'. We can be sure that, in this county of 'selig' or holy Suffolk, there were many who followed in honour of Our Lady.

. . . they went out at the West Door, through the whole length of St Peter's Street, through St Nicholas' Street, past the house where the Cardinal was born, cross the Butter-market, then by the Herb-market, then over the Corn-hill, past the Market-cross and the Town-hall, once St Mildred's Church, through St Matthew's Street, under the West-gate and to the Chapel of the famous Image.

This pilgrimage therefore takes its place with that of Our Lady of Walsingham.

On the 16th May 1695 it was agreed that any freeman suffering any foreigner to sell upon his premises, any grocery, books, pictures, or other wares, he shall forfeit his freedom; and any inn-keeper supplying the same, shall forfeit his licence.

September 1787, John Howard, the philanthropist, paid a visit to the town, and staid two days inspecting our gaols, of which he expressed the highest satisfaction.

I rather like this one:

On 19th August, the Turkish ambassador and suite passed through this town, on the way to Yarmouth. About two miles from Colchester, one of the carriages broke down; when His Excellency ordered the whole party to stop, and retired with his attendants, into an adjoining wood; where a canopy was thrown across some trees, under which he regaled himself with his pipe, for upwards of two hours, while the carriage was repairing.

21st November 1828. The members of the Friendly Society held their eighteenth anniversary, upon the town hall; and the following statement will evince the peculiar excellence of this benevolent institution: 984 bushels of coal have been carried to the houses of 123 aged persons, the majority of whom were above seventy-five years of age – one at the advanced age of a hundred, 1174 bushels of coals, 60 sheets, 135 calico garments, 232 flannel ditto, 67½ yards of flannel, and 19 yards of calico.

19th December 1828. The tenth anniversary of another excellent institution, called the Penny Club, took place here; which exhibited the pleasing spectacle of between five and six hundred children, all habited in comfortable garments, in consequence of the judicious expenditure of the funds of this society, arising principally from the savings of the poor.

May 1724. The Ipswich Spaw Waters is now opened by Mrs Martha Coward, and Attendance will be given every Morning at the Bath on St Margaret's Green, from six to nine at 1d. per Morning, and 2d. for each Falk carried off.

2nd September 1769 William Jackson having purchased the moiety of the Ipswich Journal of Mrs Elizabeth Craighton, the partnership between them was dissolved; and it was afterwards printed by him only. This lady died in February 1796 at the advanced age of ninety-two.

We end with the assessment of the character of one of its citizens.

George Frost was born at Barrow, in this county, and died at Ipswich, 28th June 1821, in the seventy-eighth year of his age; he was for many years in a confidential situation in the Old Blue coach-office; where, by his care and industry, he realized a comfortable competency for himself and his wife in his latter days. He was shy and reserved to strangers, honourable and upright in all his dealings, and was a truly independent man, enthusiastically devoted to the study of his art, which he followed at his leisure hours, from a very early period of his life. It is evident that Gainsborough was his model, but he studied nature with the closest attention, and many of his productions, particularly his drawings, were of distinguished excellence; his efforts were unaided by instruction, but he became a delightful artist by the power of his native talent alone and in many instances displayed touches of genius worthy of a master's hand, and there are few of the picturesque beauties of the vicinity of this town but what have been sketched in a bold and masterly manner by his pencil.

His genius lov'd his County's native views,
Its taper spires, green lawns, and shelter'd farms;
He touch'd each scene with nature's genuine hues,
And gave the Suffolk landscape all its charms.

He possessed a small collection of paintings, and many valuable drawings of his favourite Gainsborough; some of whose pictures he had so correctly copied, that it is said in one instance, that Gainsborough himself would not distinguish his own production. He lived respected and esteemed, and died universally lamented; and he will be long remembered as an artist, who was an honour to the town of Ipswich.

Some of his paintings are in the Christchurch Museum Art Gallery.

21

My Museum

Most people collect things nowadays – stamps, cigarette cards, bottles, coins, first editions and almost anything you can think of; but I must have started in a big way and mine became a museum. I am not quite sure how I started, but I think it was in the nature of Suffolk bygones and many of the pieces are shown in my *Household and Country Crafts*. I might also mention I was at the opening of the Reading museum and that at Stowmarket. It was great fun looking for treasures – and finding them.

My museum was housed, fittingly enough, in an old railway carriage at Westleton. The Great Eastern Railway Company in the old days used to sell off their old carriages and many of them were made into quite nice little bungalows. However, my venture grew and grew until it came into the house and would have put us into the street, like the camel and the tent. I was glad when a pen friend in New York, took most of it off my shoulders. But the small things I kept, and thereby hangs a tale. A few things went to Stowmarket.

One day I received a letter asking if I would take a small collection of toys. I demurred at first, but found the donor wanted them to go into safe keeping, as a home of long standing was being broken up. Imagine our astonishment when they arrived to find that most of them were in their original boxes. I could not but ask why that had come about. The answer was: "The toys have given much pleasure to two generations. There were four boys and three girls in my generation and we did not have access to the more breakable toys, which were served out two at a time only, for an hour before bedtime – a sound scheme by which we never had time to get tired of them. But of course, we don't see all the ones that were smashed, no doubt the majority."

First then the Walking Doll, which must be none other than Queen Victoria herself. It dates from 1862, the year after the death of the Prince Consort. She wears a crinoline of lavender silk trimmed with lace. Her head is of china, her arms and hands of washleather, and her legs and feet of pure gold. She walks rather mincingly, propelled by a splendid clockwork movement. And she was made in Germany, the then home of toys.

Still keeping with the wonderful old Queen, is a remarkable toy labelled the 'Artist', complete with box. By turning a handle the clown traces on a piece of paper pinned to the easel a drawing of the Queen's head, complete with her characteristic little crown. It is quite breathless to watch the moving pencil, which having finished its task ends with a jerk.

But I do like the old-English-penny tin toy of the 'Steam Tramway Company'. It is a splendid survival, complete with winding stairway for an upper deck that is not there. It has a magnificent circular boiler and the simulated smoke; but there is no provision for a driver.

My favourite appears at first sight to be a dull little box: $6\frac{3}{4}$ ins long by $2\frac{1}{2}$ ins wide and $1\frac{3}{4}$ ins high. Midway along the top is a hinge that enables the box to be turned back on itself. This done, a series of lavender steps appear, and at the base in a drawer are two gaily coloured tumblers, one is yellow the other blue. They possess rather long splayed feet. If placed upright on the top platform they will make a marvellous head-over-heels performance until they reach the bottom. This is made possible by a little weight in the hollow uprights that give the right momentum for the turnover.

The amicable elephant, still in its box, bears the inscription: "With Aunt Hattie's love to Helen". Does not that convey the aura of the 'seventies? On some snowy Christmas morning it must have shuffled down a slope for the first time, as it will still do when placed upright. It measures $3\frac{1}{2}$ ins long, but longer if the tail is included.

A French Example is 'Le Gai Violiniste'. The instructions are: "In order to make this pretty toy work, wind it up and place the fiddler horizontally on an even surface." Whereupon he plays and shuffles his feet. Judging by his long hair and tail coat one would take him for a *maestro*, but I do not think a master in those days would have worn check trousers on the concert platform. So we must class him among the vagrants.

The singing bird is a little masterpiece. One blows through a rubber tube, that causes the bird to whistle, its tail to flap and its beak to open and close.

The year 1962 saw the tercentenary of the appearance in England of Punch and Judy (Thomas Smythe of Ipswich (1825–1906) painted such a scene outside the Stag's Head at Ipswich). This is a sand toy in which Punch, and Judy with her baby, dance to the fiddle of Toby.

The figures attached to wires are set in motion by means of fine sand loose within the box. By turning the toy upside down, the sand is sifted into a paper hopper at the top and then trickles through a pinhole into the paddles of a wheel – exactly the same action as an over-shot water wheel. This causes the wheel to revolve to a very pleasant clucking sound.

The musical box, just 3 ins in diameter, plays "Hold the fort for I am coming", with a flourish that I am certain neither Moody nor Sankey ever intended.

Which brings us to the dolls' house, with its delightfully inconsequential view into the private life of dolls, or their owners. It reflects the homes of the period by the awful wallpaper, with no regard to proportion, from the kitchen to the servants' quarters under the roof; passing the nursery *en route*. Everything is there for comfort and cleanliness, including miniature hotwater bottles, chamber pots, baths, washstands with ware; and the inevitable four-poster, or tent bedstead.

My example is of very early Victorian vintage, on three

floors. Brussels carpet, that could only be destroyed by moth, adds comfort to the over-furnished rooms, that make not the slightest concession to the saving of labour. But as Dickens observes: "Others could be fitted on the most expensive scale, at a moment's notice, from whole shelves of chairs, tables, sofas, bedsteads and upholstery."

We might end with Cowper's lines, himself one of the world's immortal children:

> Men deal with life as children with their play,
> Who first misuse, then cast their toys away.

Needless to say, these did not go to America.

22

Return to Depden

When the noises of children are heard on the green
And laughing is heard on the hill.
William Blake.

The chapter on Depden in my last book has called forth a delightful letter about a family who lived on Depden Green named Isaacson. They came from good stock and lived at Landwade Hall near Newmarket, probably hailing originally from Luxembourg. The writer states that a William Isaacson was her great-grandfather, and his daughter Penelope her grandmother. The latter suggests a pretty face, a poke bonnet or leghorn hat and a high-waisted dress. Her own mother was born in 1876.

Needless to say that great-grandfather Isaacson was deeply annoyed when both his daughters married men he considered beneath them in station. Penelope married a John Hunt and Louise Zachariah, both sons of Robert Hunt who founded the firm of Robert Hunt & Co., Atlas Works, Earls Colne, Essex. William Isaacson called them hog-trough makers. One can trace the scorn in his voice and his feelings of contempt. (Incidentally my mother would use the word *hog* in like manner.) Perhaps William would not have been so superior if he could have known that a later descendant of Robert Hunt was to leave his entire fortune of some £500,000 to the village.

But William was no stalwart in face of danger or discomfort. He would call his wife to deal with the children when they needed correction and punishment. In fact the writer denounces him as a gutless old man. One night when a noise downstairs caused some alarm, it was his wife who had to go to investigate. She discovered a picture had fallen down and that nothing worse had occurred. When she arrived back in the bedroom, however, she found the hero had barricaded himself in by means of a chair at the door.

When Corder, of the Red Barn murder at Polstead (Suffolk's one great melodrama) was hanged, William rode into Bury St Edmunds to witness the great sight. But the crowds, the food and fruit vendors were too much for his nerves and taste, so he turned his horse homewards again.

Another instance of his gutlessness was when he saw the first train pull into the new Bury St Edmund's station. He only went to London once by train and was so terrified that he never went in a train again.

Penelope must have been a pretty little girl for a portrait of her survives, taken in 1858 when she was seven. In those days the photographer called at the house by appointment, and on this occasion, just before he was due, the girl's governess told Penelope to go into the garden and pick a little bunch of flowers to hold. The man tinted these flowers and the faint pink colour can still be seen.

When she was a very little girl she used to sit in church on a hassock at her mother's knee. A wife of one of the farm workers had a mentally defective son who used to wet himself in church. On the way out his mother would shout at him, "You dirty young dog, you! You dirty young dog!"

There is also another photograph of her, enlarged from the original, when she was sixteen or seventeen. The writer's mother was able to tell her that Penelope (*her* mother) had told her that she was wearing a new dress of royal-blue material, trimmed with cream Prussian braid. She was a small girl, not very tall, but very upright and when she went to church in this new dress an old farm worker standing in the porch said, "Pick up your skirts, Miss Penelope!" I wonder how he pronounced her name, a bit of a mouthful for a Suffolk boor.

One or two memories of this little miss survive. When she was quite a small girl, her parents had promised to take her to Bury St Edmunds with them. But she had been naughty, so they told her she must stay at home. Not to be outdone, she went to the stables, saddled her pony and was waiting for her parents when they arrived at Bury.

Another little episode was when she was crossing Depden Green. A gander came at her hissing in a rather frightening manner. Nothing loath she picked him up by the neck, swung him round and round until he was dizzy and then dropped him. Indeed, her courage stood her in good stead after she was married, for she was left a widow with six children under the age of twelve.

The local rector when Penelope was a child was old Parson Lloyd, somewhat of a character, who even in those later years wore a full-bottomed wig. He found himself in prison for debt, but the first Sunday after he was out again he was back in his pulpit. He was apparently a specialist in wives, the second of whom suffered from the scourge of lupus – a tuberculous skin disease – and her poor face was so disfigured that she always wore a lace veil to cover it. Her tombstone is in the churchyard.

Lloyd used to sit the little girl on his knee and say, "You shall be my third wife, Pen." I wonder what she wore when she married her John?

The family washing at Depden Green was done once a month only and wood ash would be placed in the letch bucket and water poured on. This produced a washing lye in which the clothes were washed. The women would have worn pattens, the click-clack of which made a pretty noise over the cobbles. And they could tell by the sound of these clogs whether it was one of the young ones, or an older worker. The beds in the house were four-posters and were so high off the ground that little steps had to be climbed to get into them.

Evidently there were plenty of characters about that old farmhouse. One of the old men who lived in one of the farm buildings used to come into the kitchen for his meals. He used a wooden spoon that hung up by the fireplace. If it happened to be missing he would exclaim, "Gal! where's my garpin spoon?" A good old Suffolk word, surely, and Forby has it – "A gape or garpe stick, a large wooden spoon".

When old William felt a bit peckish he would 'fry a froise', which is another Suffolk word for a pancake. In his case eaten with fat pork!

Penelope is buried in Earls Colne churchyard, just opposite the house, Rose Cottage, where she brought up her children. It is now the local vicarage. The writer adds, "I spent weeks on end there with her, and was, I know, spoilt by her, for I was her first grandchild and could do no wrong."

The Isaacsons were buried at Depden churchyard, and the writer says she visited there just over twenty years ago and was fortunate to see the old verger, who was locking up after the monthly afternoon service. The church is approached by crossing or by walking round the edge of a field. She asked him about the Isaacson vault, and he remembered seeing a man whitewashing the interior. The entrance is now silted up and the key lost. Time has grown over it – "impatient to destroy".

(My informant, Dr. Doreen Penelope Firmin, died February 2, 1979.)

23

Great Glemham

The red-breast whistles from a garden-croft;
And gathering swallows twitter in the sky.
John Keats

One can gather the pride in the simple statement, "I was born in the village of Great Glemham in 1897". Understandable, when accompanied by an old photograph (*see* plate 12), so full of memories and soft outlines; the Suffolk of yesterday. Bridge Street, spanning the little trickle of a stream known as the Ore, which goes on and on so silently until it joins the Alde at Snape. Curiously enough the writer's maiden name was Bridge, the youngest of a large family and the last survivor. The two supporters of the old brick culvert were the oldest members of the village, and the little chapel on the left was the one her father attended.

It is in reality a lovely letter, full of old half-forgotten things. Her father was a small-holder and tenant of the Duke of Hamilton, and managed to carry on when the large estate was broken up. "I remember so well the Duke's only daughter, Lady Mary Hamilton, visiting the village school before her marriage to Lord Graham, and presenting each child with a charming pewter mug inscribed with her initials and dated 1905. I still have it and treasure it. Miss Geater [a good old Suffolk name] was the head-mistress of the school.

"The Woolnoughs were tenant farmers, and a Mrs Woolnough, a widow in the village, sold pork from her cottage. My father always went down to help her cut up the pork and prepare for the sausage making. She also sold scraps. The taste and smell lingers in the memory, as well they might. Now back to the old photograph, and note the old grit road.

"The cottage on the left is where we lived for a time. The house opposite is the Old Parsonage, where my mother's old friend, Miss Aldis came to live when she retired as Matron from the Middlesex Hospital. They were peaceful happy days." Need one say more, for the scene is full of felicitations and a cloudless Suffolk countryside in high summer.

But there is another glory in Great Glemham, and that is the Church of All Saints, and the glory of that church is one of Suffolk's seven-sacrament fonts; a lovely thing, God wot. It stands on a pedestal, the stem decorated with pots of lilies. What artists there were in those Catholic days! It seems to vie with the one at Cratfield. The panels represent ordination, penance, mass, extreme unction, the crucifixion, confirmation, marriage and baptism. And this is what Munro Cautley has to say about it:

> Quite apart from the fact that all the panels have a rayed background as at Woodbridge and Denston, notice the exorcized devil in the penance panel, the altar with chalice and canopy above the mass panel and, most interesting of all, are the chrismataries shown in the panels depicting extreme unction and confirmation. These exactly conform to the existing examples at St Martin's Canterbury, and Granborough Church, Bucks, where the box has a steep pitched lid like the roof of a house and contains three small pots holding the holy oils of liturgical use *oleum infirmorum* for the sick, *oleum sanctum*, used at baptisms, and the *chrisma* or balm used at confirmation, ordination and generally at consecrations.

The Church has a north porch which contains a stoop for holy water with a cusped arch; and the nave has an arch-braced roof. Three Brasyer bells of the fifteenth century are inscribed (in translation): "*May this ring be blessed by the good offices of the*

Baptist. I am when rung called Mary, the Rose of the world. This bell is made in the praise of good saints." Not a bad composition for one small village. I wonder if those bells still give out their essential English music over those peaceful fields, and the quiet acre that holds so much of Great Glenham's past.

Because it has a past, described thus: "The manor is all freehold and did belong, with the rectoral tithes, to Butley Priory, and afterwards to the Edgar family." Besides it has a Poads farm, whatever that means. When W. White compiled his directory in 1844 the village contained a saddler, thatcher, tailor, two blacksmiths, two boot and shoemakers, twelve farmers, three shopkeepers, two wheelwrights. And William Robinson kept the Crown Inn.

"About 22 acres of land has, from an early period, been appropriated to the repair of the church and the relief of the poor, and is now let for £28 per annum, with some cottages, formerly the parish workhouse." And here lived the Rev. George Crabbe for some four or five years in 1796.

It should be mentioned that Crabbe became rector of Muston in Leicestershire and the neighbouring parish of Allington in Lincolnshire in 1789. In 1791 he visited Parham and neighbouring Suffolk villages and returned to Muston in 1792. Recalled to Parham on the death of his father-in-law, Mr Tovell, he placed a curate at Muston. He then undertook the charge of Sweffling for the incumbent, the Rev Richard Turner of Great Yarmouth. The curacy of Great Glemham was also added.

Great Glemham Hall, a house belonging to Mr North, became vacant and was offered to Crabbe at a greatly reduced rent. He moved in to this beautiful residence where he remained for four or five years. And this is what his son said about the place.

> . . . association of our happiest years are all with Glemham. . . Glemham itself is, and ever will be, the Alhambra of my imagination. A small well wooded park occupied the whole mouth of the

glen, whence, doubtless, the name of the village was derived. In the lowest ground stood the commodious mansion; the approach wound down through the plantation on the eminence in front. The opposite hill rose at the back of it, rich and varied with trees and shrubs scattered irregularly; under this southern hill ran a brook, and on the banks above were spots of great natural beauty, crowned by whitethorn and oak. Here the purple-scented violet perfumed the air, and in one place coloured the ground. On the left of the front, in the narrower portion of the glen, was the village; on the right, a confined view of richly wooded fields. In fact, the whole parish and neighbourhood resemble a combination of groves, interspersed with fields cultivated like gardens, and intersected with those green dry lanes which tempt the walker in all weathers, especially in the evenings, when in the short grass of the dry sandy banks lies every few yards a glow-worm, and the nightingales are pouring forth their melody in every direction.

Again, the son tells of walks among those woods, going home: ". . . while on the right and left, before and behind, the nightingales (I have never heard so many as among those woods) were pouring out their melody, sometimes three or four at once. And now we fill the margin of our hats with glow-worms to place upon the lawn before our windows, and reach the house in time for supper."

Whilst at Glemham the Rev. George continued his practice of treating his poor parishioners free of charge, not forgetting his love of herbal remedies. And it was whilst here that he completed *The Parish Register*:

The year revolves, and I again explore
The simple annals of my parish poor;
. . . .
Behold the cot! where thrives th' industrious swain,
Source of his pride, his pleasure, and his gain;
Screen'd from the winter's wind, the sun's last ray
Smiles on the window and prolongs the day;
Projecting thatch, the woodbine's branches stop,
And turn their blossoms to the casement's top:

Curiously enough, when the bishops began to urge non-resident incumbents to return to their livings, it was Dr Pretty-man, Bishop of Lincoln, grandfather of Felixstowe's noted Colonel Tomline, who refused to allow Crabbe to remain in Suffolk.

24

The Constable Affair

In a letter to Archdeacon Fisher, 23rd October 1821, Constable wrote:

> . . . How I wish I had been with you on your fishing excursion in the New Forest! . . . As long as I do paint, I shall never cease to paint such places. . . . Still I should paint my own places best; painting is with me but another name for feeling, and I associate "my careless boyhood" with all that lies on the banks of the Stour; those scenes made me a painter, and I am grateful; that is, I had often thought of pictures of them before I ever touched a pencil, and your picture is the strongest instance of it I can recollect; but I will say no more, for I am a great egoist in whatever relates to painting.

The art world, and Suffolk in particular, were suddenly confronted with the rather startling news that some of John Constable's paintings were not by him at all, but by his fourth son Lionel. One particular picture being the best-loved painting "Near Stoke by Nayland", now hanging in the Tate Gallery.

The discovery, a remarkable piece of work, was made by Mr Leslie Parris, deputy keeper of the Tate Gallery, and Mr Ian Flemming-Williams the art historian. They have proved so far, that fourteen individual paintings and sketches, as well as an entire sketch book, attributed to Constable are by his son Lionel Bicknell Constable. Their studies vindicated the 100 paintings and 300 drawings by Constable presented by Isabel, his second daughter and herself a flower painter, to the Victoria and Albert Museum in 1880.

Three other sons painted – John Charles, Charles Golding and Alfred. A grandson, Hugh, painted marine and country scenes. Lionel Constable, born in 1828 was aged nine when his father died. He painted marine and country pictures until he took an interest in the new art of photography after 1852.

The two art historians have examined a wide range of Constable's work, which is invariably unsigned, for evidence of the hand of Lionel or Alfred, the artist's third son who expressed worry in letters that his painting was too like his father's.

Mr Legatt said that the confusion between Lionel was only the tip of the iceberg. After all, Constable was the most imitated and faked British artist in the nineteenth century.

A leading article, at the time of the discovery, in the *Daily Telegraph* speaks of the breathtakingly ingenious scholarship that has established beyond reasonable doubt the work of Lionel, and goes on: "No one can be blamed. There is no master forger cowering in the wings. Possibly Hugh Constable, who sold a vast number of paintings purporting to be by his grandfather, could tell us a thing or two, but he is long dead."

But it must be stated in his defence that when Hugh sold the pictures in 1890 there was not a good market for them, although the family was in great need of money. One cannot enter into the technical details of the difference between the master and his son. But a letter in the *Daily Telegraph*, headed "A Star is Born in Art", seems to me to sum up the matter for the average layman.

The news that a number of works hitherto attributed to John Constable – and duly venerated and valued as such – are not by the master after all, but by his youngest child Lionel Bicknell Constable, will come as a shock to some galleries, collectors and dealers who will sustain a loss of face as well as capital diminution.

Their loss is, surely, the community's gain, for this discovery is most exciting – rather like the identification of a new star in the firmament.

The fact that the famous pastoral scene entitled "Near Stoke by Nayland" in the Tate, is by Lionel and not by John Constable, detracts nothing from its beauty, its general competence, its fine composition or the pleasure it gives to thousands. Its market value may be slashed at a stroke, but its value in real terms is unimpaired.

It is perhaps, unfortunate that the Constables failed to oblige investors by signing and dating their works, but the remarkable research carried out by Mr Parris and Mr Flemming-Williams has remedied an injustice by elevating Lionel from obscurity to recognition overnight and another name is added to the many eminent Victorian painters. They deserve our thanks.

The fact that Lionel Constable is now shown to be a very competent painter will do nothing to damage the reputation of the father or the affection accorded him by the public; rather it will add a touch of piquancy and interest to an otherwise well-documented family.

25

Aldeburgh

There is no sea like the Aldeburgh sea; it talks to me.
Edward FitzGerald

Millicent Fawcett, in *What I Remember*, draws this charming vignette of her birthplace: "I remember walking along the Crag Path at Aldeburgh (we always resisted with vehemence any Cockney attempt to call it The Esplanade, The Parade, or any such name) when I was young enough to be holding my father's hand and hearing him and listening with all my ears to his arguments while he was persuading some of the leaders among the beachmen to volunteer for the Navy at the beginning of the Crimea War."

The Crag Path has epitomized Aldeburgh through all the long years, giving this delightful resort its Cranford-like atmosphere. How lovely it was when I was a boy to arrive at the terminus on the branch line of the old Great Eastern Railway from Saxmundham, with an eight-day return ticket for eight shillings and walk towards the sea in the peaceful sunlit days of a horse-drawn Suffolk.

The very first thing to note was the post windmill just round the corner from the station. One could almost hear its deep breath if it happened to be at work. Then, as one approached Church Hill there was Hall Farm on the left and Albert Brewery on the right, both under the same ownership. I can remember the lovely smell of malt and hops which pervaded the air and the barrels and kegs about the entrance that seemed to perpetuate the smuggling memories when Crabbe's father was the Customs Officer.

As one reached the brow of the hill there was the sea, and the old Moot Hall standing like a stranded hulk on the shingle. And Aldeburgh was full of all kinds of romantic and interesting people. There were pilots, master mariners, fishermen, all bearing local names. Not forgetting Newson Garrett, maltster, corn and coal merchant, who fell out with everyone in turn, his own brother the ironmaster at Leiston included; but was the bravest of the brave.

Neither should we forget that it was his forceful character that saw his daughter through the loophole that the Society of Apothecaries provided to make her the first woman doctor to graduate in this country. The medical profession was a closed shop in those days, and the Society suddenly realized what this persistent young woman was after and tried to slam the door. But they were too late because father stormed and threatened. Members of that family now lie in an enclosure of their own on the north side of the church.

About midway along the Crag Path was the lifeboat station, with a splendid vessel ever at the ready. Before you got as far as that came the Jubilee Hall, with that long list of vessels to the aid of which those brave men had gone. Then, before we made our way back to the station, we would visit the memorial in the churchyard, to the seven men who were drowned by the capsizing of their boat on 7th December 1899. It appears they were launching from the beach when they got stuck on a sandbank and in trying to get it off overturned the boat.

Of course Aldeburgh has changed somewhat during the decades. The station and railway have gone, the windmill also, and the brewery. Yet Aldeburgh retains its atmosphere of culture and refinement because another name has arisen, or should we say two, Benjamin Britten and Peter Pears. It is unlike anywhere else, soothing and beneficent – a delightful place indeed.

In a recent visit I went to that rather large churchyard to

visit a new grave, bearing this simple inscription; "Benjamin Britten 1913–1976". My thoughts went to another such grave in Grasmere bearing the words "William Wordsworth. Born 1770. Died 1850". I was told by a local inhabitant with a Suffolk accent that that was what Benjamin Britten wanted, because he was 'just like that'. I did not fail to notice that someone had planted a small fuchsia, the bush that stood pre-eminent in old cottage gardens; how appropriate.

But that churchyard held something else for me, two members of the Barham family, connected in service with the Garrett family. I was directed to their grave by an old sailor busy at work mowing the long grass. He knew that churchyard and, I felt sure loved it, so we talked for a moment of that lifeboat memorial. He said his grandmother went into the water on that awful night, pulled out a survivor, then went in again and pulled out another. A fortnight after she had a baby. Surely that was the Aldeburgh spirit. I noticed also the tattoo marks on his arm that linked him with the sea and I thought how lucky I was to meet him. So he helped me copy out the inscription I was after.

"In Respectful and Affectionate Memory of Samuel Barham who died at Aldeburgh Jan. 30, 1899 aged 87. Fifty eight years of his life were spent in one of friendship and service the memory is treasured by the family to whom he devoted them. HE WAS A FAITHFUL MAN, AND FEARED GOD ABOVE MANY." My sailor friend said he liked the penultimate sentence.

Next was a duplicate stone: "Also in memory of SCIPPIA, who for over sixty years was the loving wife of Samuel Barham, she died September 13, 1900. 'There is sprung up a light for the righteous and gladness for such as are pure hearted.'" Samuel Barham was my grandfather's cousin, a great character and Scippia was even more so.

I once went to see Benjamin Britten about a little booklet I was writing and when I sent two copies this is what he wrote: "Thank you very much for sending Mr. Pears and me copies of your Aldeburgh book which we have looked at with great pleasure. It is full of most interesting information, and extremely well laid out. I am sure you will have a great success with it, and you can be certain we will do all we can to let people know about it."

I happen to possess a brochure of the first Aldeburgh Festival, which, please note, was priced 1d. The festival lasted a week, 5th, 13th June 1948, and I give a list of the items with those taking part:

Opera in the Jubilee Hall. The English Opera Group presents *Albert Herring* by Benjamin Britten, with Joan Cross, Peter Pears, Nancy Evans, Otakar Kraus, Margaret Ritchie, Dennis Dowling, Catherine Lawson, Gladys Parr, Roy Ashton, Norman Lumsden.

Choral and Orchestral Concert in the parish Church.

Saint Nicholas. A Cantata. Words by Eric Crozier, music by Benjamin Britten, with Peter Pears (tenor) and string orchestra. The Aldeburgh Festival Choir.

Recital in the Cinema. Clifford Curzon, pianoforte. This recital included the Piano Sonata by Lennox Berkeley.

Recital in the Parish Church. Peter Pears and Benjamin Britten. A recital including Elizabethan songs, Purcell, Schubert and Britten.

Recital in the Parish Church. The Zorian String Quartet. Olive Zorian, Winifred Copperwheat, Norina Semino, Marjorie Lavers, with Stephen Waters (clarinet) Benjamin Britten (pianoforte).

Concert in the Jubilee Hall. The English Opera Group Chamber Orchestra.

Verse and Music in the Parish Church. Dame Edith Evans (engagements permitting), Celia Johnson, Robert Speaight.

Tuesday 8th June. Poetry of the Bible with interludes of vocal and organ music.

Two Popular Concerts. Saturday 12th June in the Jubilee Hall. Sunday 13th June in the Cinema. A programme of popular vocal duets, trios and quartets, including Liza Lehmann's "In a Persian Garden".

Lectures in the Baptist Chapel.

Monday 7th June. E. M. Forster on George Crabbe and "Peter Grimes".

Tuesday 8th June William Plomer on Edward FitzGerald.

Wednesday 9th June. Geoffrey Grigson on "Crabbe – The Romantic Poet".

Thursday 10th June. Tyrone Guthrie on "The Theatre today".

Friday 11th June. Sir Kenneth Clarke on "East Anglian Painting".

I notice that in the Programme Book costing 5s., Tyrone Guthrie is given for Wednesday, and that on the Thursday Stuart Wilson is given to speak on "The Future of Music". Geoffrey Grigson is not on the list.

It is not without interest that the Festival followed in the steps of the noted Newson Garrett, from Aldeburgh to Snape Maltings. It was confined to Aldeburgh for its 'first'.

Postscript

It would seem to me that this present decade is noted for three things. First the creation of new museums, especially of the rural-bygone type; second a growing interest in family genealogy, be it ever so humble; third the amazing scramble for old photographs, even to early picture postcards. In all these regions Suffolk and East Anglia maintain a good share.

This is particularly so in old photographs, when one considers that it was a doctor, Peter Henry Emerson, living at Southwold who produced the most coveted of them all. In 1886 he published a volume containing forty of his platinotype pictures, entitled *Life and Landscape on the Norfolk Broads*, priced originally at £6 6s. One of these created something of a sensation when it fetched the extraordinary sum of £12,000 at Christie's in 1976. Needless to say it went to America, and any succeeding copies sent to the sale rooms likewise.

Then, this year, 1978, the Ipswich Record Office managed to secure an album of early Victorian photographs taken about 1850, including studies of the Ipswich Ragged School and nearby pictures of Ipswich subjects, for £2,200. Other groups went to America.

These were taken by Richard Dyke Alexander, a Quaker and member of the Suffolk bankers, Alexander and Co. He was connected with Fox Talbot, which might explain the quality of his work. Incidentally, it was at the Woodbridge branch of this bank that Bernard Barton worked.

Victoriana seems to evoke a charm nowadays, looking

backwards rather than forwards to what looks like a faceless age of the computer. Perhaps a little five-year old boy stumbled on the right answer when, according to a note in the *Daily Telegraph* he asked for 'A News of the Next World', please.

Sound advice is also reported by a reader of the *Daily Telegraph* in a cautious notice at an unmanned East Anglian level crossing: "Give Way to Trains".